A REASONED DEFENSE OF THE FAITH

Published by:
1517 Academic, an imprint of 1517 Publishing
PO Box 54032
Irvine, CA 92619-4032

Publisher's Cataloging-In-Publication Data
(Prepared by Cassidy Cataloguing, Inc.)

Names: Francisco, Adam, author.
Title: A reasoned defense of the faith : collected essays in Christian apologetics / Adam S. Francisco.
Description: Irvine, CA : 1517 Academic, an imprint of 1517 Publishing, [2026] | Includes bibliographical references and index.
Identifiers: ISBN: 9781964419879 (paperback) | 9781964419886 (ebook)
Subjects: LCSH: Apologetics. | Bible—Evidences, authority, etc. | Jesus Christ—Resurrection. | Natural law—Religious aspects—Christianity. | Christianity and other religions. | LCGFT: Essays. | BISAC: RELIGION / Essays. | RELIGION / Christian Theology / Apologetics.
Classification: LCC: BT1103 .F73 2026 | DDC: 239—dc23

Printed in the United States of America.

Cover art by Zachariah James Stuef.

We are grateful to *The Evangelical Church of England, Christian Education, Concordia Theological Quarterly, Concordia Publishing House, Logia,* and *Modern Reformation* for their cooperation and permission to include previously published materials from their periodicals in this volume.

The essay *Natural Law: A Basis for Christian-Muslim Discourse* is taken from *Natural Law: A Lutheran Reappraisal* © 2011 Concordia Publishing House. Used with permission. All rights reserved. cph.org.

ACADEMIC

A REASONED DEFENSE OF THE FAITH

COLLECTED ESSAYS IN CHRISTIAN APOLOGETICS

—

ADAM S. FRANCISCO

Contents

Introduction

The New Testament encourages Christians scattered among non-believers to always be ready to give a reason—an apologetic—for the hope that is found in Christ (1 Pt. 3:15). It is, therefore, interesting that in some circles of Christianity, apologetic training and thinking are all but absent. There are any number of reasons for this. They can range anywhere from a general apathy towards any sort of engagement with critical unbelievers to a theological rejection of the utility of the endeavor. The one thing they all have in common, though, is their ambivalence towards the study and practice of Christian apologetics, despite the exhortation to be ready and able to do it in Peter's first epistle.

The church owes the world an apology—a reasonable defense, explanation, and even a positive case for its claims—lest it be ignored or critiqued as just another cleverly devised myth (2 Pt. 3:16). In the past, the church has, in fact, given reasons. There is a tremendous legacy of apologetic activity throughout its history—from St. Paul in Athens and before Agrippa (Acts 17 and 26) to C.S. Lewis's "Case for Christianity" in his BBC Broadcast Talks in the middle of World War II. Early church fathers like Justin Martyr and Athenagoras of Athens wrote apologies addressed to persecuting Roman senators and emperors. Medieval scholars and missionaries such as Thomas Aquinas and Riccoldo da Monte di Croce addressed Muslim objections to the gospel. And thinkers through the modern era like the father of international law, Hugo Grotius, and current emeritus Professor of Mathematics at Oxford, John Lennox, have all heeded the call to be prepared to answer the criticisms and questions of their day and to give reasons illustrating the reasonableness of their faith in Christ.

The call to and practice of apologetics has been and will remain relevant wherever the gospel is resisted. This is especially the case in America, where Christianity is often in the crosshairs of secular culture. Atheistic material ridicules it. The ever-increasing presence of Islam asserts its supremacy over it. And popular influencers use and manipulate scholarly research to deconstruct it. This list could go on, but you get the picture. The bottom line is, according to the sainted John Warwick Montgomery,

> [W]e need to return to our biblical and theological foundations to find the place which apologetics should have in Christian ministry. That place is absolutely clear. We are to do as the Apostle did: "While Paul waited for them at Athens, his spirit was stirred in him when he saw the city wholly given to idolatry. Therefore he disputed in the synagogue with the Jews…and in the market daily with them that met with him, and with certain philosophers of the Epicureans and of the Stoics…. We are to become "all things to all people, that some might be saved, a Jew to the Jew and a Greek to the Greeks," which necessarily entails giving reasons for the faith…. We must not reduce the faith once delivered to the saints to a cultic matter of inner experience and personal testimony. There are enough irrational religions and sects in our 21st-century world without giving the unbeliever the impression that Christianity is just another one of them.[1]

The essays and articles in this little volume are all, to one degree or another, committed to advancing the apologetic task (though the first might better be described as more of a polemic). They are not definitive. That would require a much larger and more specialized book. Instead, they are a collection of relatively short apologetic writings drawn together from a variety of sources. All but one of them has been published elsewhere (see acknowledgments below) and, in most cases, quite some time ago. Some minor corrections and changes have been made, but they all reflect what was originally published. They can be read independently of each other or

---

[1] John Warwick Montgomery, "Apologetics for the 21st Century," in *Christ as Centre and Circumference: Essays Theological, Cultural and Polemic* (Bonn: Verlag für Kultur und Wissenschaft, 2012), 136-137.

somewhat sequentially. The intention was to provide a source (but not a primary source) book for thinking about various apologetic topics, which could be used for personal study or for a reading or study group, perhaps even a class on Christian apologetics. In fact, that is the hope.

Acknowledgments

Some of the essays contained in this book have appeared in print before. The author thanks the original publishers for their kind and prompt permission to reprint them here for easier access and broader dissemination.

"Authority: The Holy Scriptures," in *Where Christ Is Present*, eds. John Warwick Montgomery and Gene Edward Veith (Irvine: New Reformation Press, 2015), 65-78.

"God Has Spoken through the Prophets...and by the Son: Word of God in Islam and Christianity," in *Built on the Foundation of the Apostles and Prophets: Sola Scriptura in Context*, ed. Tapani Simojoki (Cambridge: The Evangelical Church of England, 2013), 101-111.

"Positive Apologetics," *Issues in Christian Education* 46/3 (2013): 30-35.

"Luther's Use of Apologetics," *Concordia Theological Quarterly* 81 (2017): 249-261.

"Can a Historian Explain the Empty Tomb with the Resurrection of Jesus?" in *The Resurrection Fact: Responding to Modern Critics*, eds. John J. Bombaro and Adam S. Francisco (Irvine: New Reformation Publications, 2017), 43-58.

"Natural Law: A Basis for Christian-Muslim Discourse," in *Natural Law: A Lutheran Reappraisal*, eds. Robert C. Baker and Roland Dap Ehlke (St. Louis: CPH, 2011), 235-247.

"The Relevance of Islamic Theology," *Logia* 18/4 (2009): 13-17.

"Jesus, Muslims, and the Gospel," *Modern Reformation* 18/3 (2009): 26-29.

"The Challenge of the New Atheism" was originally delivered as a lecture at Concordia Theological Seminary's annual confessional symposium in 2010 under the title "The New Atheism and Its Impact."

The Authority of
the Holy Scriptures

Every theological tradition that identifies itself as Christian maintains the authority of the Scriptures in some sense of the term, and yet they all disagree on a number of issues concerning the theology (and practice) of Christianity. This is largely due to the additional authorities Christians have added alongside or on top of the authority of Scripture.

Coming to terms with biblical authority is of the utmost importance. For what one identifies as authoritative when it comes to theology ultimately informs (if not determines) where one will end up on the theological spectrum. Moreover, if theology is at its most basic level a reassertion of God's revelation to humankind expressed in the language of a particular culture, then it becomes all the more important lest Christians idolatrously elevate and confuse the words (and will) of men with the words (and will) of the Creator.

That the Christian church has always had, in one way or another, a high view of the Bible should come as no surprise. After all, God himself—in the person of Jesus—held the Hebrew Bible of his day (the Old Testament) as the ultimate theological authority. At the beginning of his ministry, when he was tempted by Satan in the wilderness, he consistently responded by appealing directly to the Bible, calling it the word of God (Matt. 4:4). At the end of his ministry, while walking with the two confused men on the way toward Emmaus, he directed them to "Moses and all the prophets" to explain the meaning of the events that had just transpired in Jerusalem. It was at this point—in the physical presence of Jesus after his crucifixion and resurrection—that those men came to see just what the prophetic message of the Old Testament really meant (Luke 24:13–35).[1]

Experiences like this are what emboldened the apostles and disciples of Jesus unwaveringly to preach the gospel, despite opposition that soon escalated into persecution. As Clement of Rome (fl. 96) explained, "Being fully assured by the resurrection of our Lord Jesus Christ, and with faith confirmed by the word of God, they went forth in the assurance of the Holy Spirit preaching the good news."[2] Jesus had commissioned them to bring the message of the gospel "to the ends of the earth" (Acts 1:8). To accomplish this, before his ascension, he promised to send them the Holy Spirit so they would be able to recall everything he taught them, guiding them in all truth (Jn. 14:15–31; 16:4–15). Eventually, after turning the world upside down with their preaching and persuasion—as the people from Thessalonica complained (Acts 17:6)—they inscribed those things to which they had been eyewitnesses, or had learned from eyewitnesses, into the texts that make up the New Testament.[3]

Certainly not everything was written down. There was too much to write about (Jn. 20:30; 21:25). Nevertheless, what was written still comprised the inspired apostolic message in all its fullness. Thus, after the generation of apostles, with their inspired teachings, had passed away, God's word remained, located in the two Testaments.

This, at least, is how the early church father Irenaeus of Lyons (d. 202) saw it in what is arguably the earliest extrabiblical source specifically addressing the issue of authority. Irenaeus wrote, "We have learned from none others the plan of salvation, than from those through whom the Gospel has come down to us, which they did at one time proclaim in public, and, at a later period, by the will of

---

[1] Quotations from the Bible are taken from the English Standard Version (Wheaton, IL: Crossway, 2001).

[2] 1 Clement 42:3., in *The Apostolic Fathers*, ed. Kirsopp Lake (New York: G. P. Putnam's Sons, 1919), 1:81.

[3] On this, see J. E. Komoszewski, M. J. Sawyer, and D. B. Wallace, *Reinventing Jesus: How Contemporary Skeptics Miss the Real Jesus and Mislead Popular Culture* (Grand Rapids, MI: Kregel Publications, 2006), 21–38.

God, handed down to us in the Scriptures, to be the ground and pillar of our faith."[4] What these words by a preeminent early church father tell us is that the texts comprising the New Testament were deemed (along with the Hebrew Bible) as the final authority for the Christian church. Irenaeus would also criticize those who placed other sources—especially oral tradition—alongside the Scriptures. He was convinced that Scripture alone was sufficient for all matters of theology. This position was normative for Christian believers of the first three centuries of the Christian era. Tertullian (160–220) and Cyprian (d. 258), for example, advanced similar claims.

A competing view of authority, however, emerged in the fourth century. Basil of Caesarea (ca. 330–70) asserted, "Of the beliefs and practices whether generally accepted or publicly enjoined which are preserved in the Church some we possess derived from written teaching; others we have received delivered to us 'in a mystery' by the tradition of the apostles; and both of these in relation to true religion have the same force."[5] And Augustine of Hippo (354–430) suggested that "there are many things which are observed by the whole Church, and therefore are fairly held to have been enjoined by the apostles, which yet are not mentioned in their writings."[6] Elsewhere, in one of the most influential of Augustine's writings, was the assertion, "I should not believe the gospel except as moved by the authority of the Catholic Church."[7] What Augustine meant in this convoluted passage is hard to determine. Some of his medieval interpreters argued that the church (and its traditions) carried only a practical or "instrumental authority." But Augustine was generally understood as proffering a view that asserted the "metaphysical priority" of the church and its tradition.[8]

---

[4] Irenaeus, *Adversus Haeresus*, in *Ante-Nicene Fathers*, ed. Philip Schaff (Peabody, MA: Hendrickson Publishers, 1996), 1:415.

[5] Basil, *De Spiritu Sancto*, in *Nicene and Post-Nicene Fathers*, ed. Philip Schaff (Peabody, MA: Hendrickson Publishers, 1996), 8:42.

[6] Augustine, *On Baptism against the Donatists*, in *Nicene and Post-Nicene Fathers*, 4:475.

[7] Augustine, *Against the Letter of Mani*, in *Nicene and Post-Nicene Fathers*, 4:131.

[8] Heiko A. Oberman, "*Quo Vadis Petre*? Tradition from Irenaeus to *Humani Generis*," in *The Dawn of the Reformation: Essays in Late Medieval and Early Reformation Thought* (Edinburgh: T&T Clark, 1992), 278.

The result was a very different understanding of the authority of the Scriptures from that held by the very earliest Christian believers—specifically that "the Christian owes equal respect and obedience to the written *and* unwritten ecclesiastical traditions, whether they are contained in the canonical writings or in the secret oral tradition handed down by the Apostles through succession."[9] One can find the latter viewpoint along with the competing, earlier theological position in the writings of a number of medieval Christians. Eventually, however, the two-source theory elevating unwritten tradition to the status of an authority alongside Scripture came to predominate.

George Tavard has argued that the position of the church having "her own revelation, independent of that which the Apostles recorded in their writings" was fully embraced by the fourteenth century.[10] Heiko Oberman, however, has challenged this and shown that the move toward the two-source approach as the dominant paradigm came earlier.[11] Already, by the twelfth century, the views of Basil and Augustine were written into canon law. It was then that "equal reverence for scriptural and extra-scriptural oral traditions" became the position of the church.[12] Oberman also noted that scholastic theologians began to justify that view by assuming a certain coinherence between the Scripture and the traditions of the church. As Henry of Ghent (1217–93) put it in his commentary on Peter Lombard's (1100–1160) *Sentences*, "The church and Holy Scripture agree in everything and testify to the same thing, namely to the truth of the faith, in which it is reasonable to believe both of them."[13] It became commonplace, then, to assume that Scripture and church tradition, even though the latter may not be found in or even deduced from Scripture, implicitly agreed with each other.

---

[9] Oberman, "*Quo Vadis Petre?*," 277.

[10] George Tavard, *Holy Writ or Holy Church?* (New York: Burns & Oates, 1959), 36.

[11] For a full exposé on the crisis of the status of Scripture, church, and tradition, see Beryl Smalley, *The Study of the Bible in the Middle Ages* (Notre Dame: Notre Dame University Press, 1964), 215ff.

[12] Oberman, "*Quo Vadis Petre?*," 277.

[13] Quoted in Carl A. Volz, *The Medieval Church: From the Dawn of the Middle Ages to the Eve of the Reformation* (Nashville: Abingdon Press, 1997), 162.

The young Martin Luther (1483–1546) seems to have inherited this position. In his first lectures on the Psalms, he remarked, "As Christ is the Head of the church, so Scripture is also the head."[14] And in his lectures on Paul's epistle to the Romans, he expressed the viewpoint thus: "The authority of the church has been established, and to this day the Roman church still holds it."[15] Early in his career, he was intent on remaining "in agreement with the Catholic church and the teachers of the church."[16] Behind these early statements, most scholars see Luther as basically assuming that the historical church and its traditions were equal in authority "alongside Scripture."[17] Given the developments in the medieval church, this is not all that surprising.

All this would change, however, shortly after Luther drafted the *Ninety-Five Theses* in the fall of 1517. In a little more than three years, as the young theologian was forced by circumstances to examine his initial presumption of a basic coherence of the Bible and the traditions of the church, he would find himself driven to Scripture alone.

The impetus for this move came when Pope Leo X (1475–1521) notified Luther that he was being tried for heresy as his *Theses* had called into question the theory and practice of indulgence sales. To explain the seriousness of what Luther had done, the pope sent, along with the Bull summoning the German monk to Rome, a document explaining the church's current view on authority. This document was written by the pope's theological adviser Sylvester Prierias (1456–1523) and titled *A Dialogue concerning the Power of the Pope*. It argued that contemporaneous teachings and practices of the church rested upon the authority of the papacy. To challenge them was to challenge his divine authority, for "neither the Church of Rome nor the Supreme Pontiff reaching his decisions as Pontiff, that is, pronouncing out of his office, and doing what is in him in order to understand the truth can err."[18] In short, the document maintained

---

[14] Jaroslav Pelikan and Helmut T. Lehmann, eds., *Luther's Works*, vol. 11 (St. Louis, MO: Concordia Publishing House, 1955ff.), 517 [hereafter cited as LW].

[15] LW 25:415.

[16] LW 31:16.

[17] Bernard Lohse, *Martin Luther's Theology: Its Historical and Systematic Development*, trans. Roy A. Harrisville (Minneapolis, MN: Fortress Press, 1999), 187.

[18] Sylvester Prierias, "Dialogus de potestate Papae," in *Documents Illustrative of the Continental Reformation*, ed. B. J. Kidd (Oxford: Clarendon Press, 1911), 31.

that the teachings of the papacy were the "infallible rule of faith."
What probably surprised Luther the most in reading this document,
however, was its claim that "holy Scriptures derived their strength
and authority" from the church.[19]

Initially, Luther did not take Prierias's argument for the priority
of the church very seriously—at least he did not think it represented
the official position of Rome.[20] But he soon found, particularly when
he stood before Cardinal Cajetan at the Diet of Augsburg (1518), that
the very opposite was the case. Luther therefore articulated his position in the following terms: "In matters of faith not only is a general
council above the pope, but also any believer, provided he uses better
authority or reason than the pope.... For the pope is not above but
under the word of God."[21] This did not mean that the pope lacked
administrative authority; Luther was simply insisting that "the truth
of Scripture must come first. After that is accepted, one may determine whether the words of men can be accepted as true."[22] Cajetan's
only response to Luther's arguments was baldly to assert the pope's
authority *over* Scripture.[23]

Eight months later, Luther advanced similar arguments in
his debate with the notorious polemicist Johann Eck at Leipzig
(1519). He then publicly set forth his position in an open letter to
Pope Leo X—affixed to his widely read *The Freedom of a Christian*
(1520). There he explained, "I never intended to attack the Roman
Curia or to raise any controversy concerning it. But when I saw
all efforts to save it were hopeless, I despised it, gave it a bill of
divorce."[24]

Luther referred to this "divorce" as having taken place before
his debate with Eck. Thus, it can be inferred that he had already

---

[19] Prierias, "Dialogus," 32.

[20] See Carter Lindberg, "Prierias and His Significance for Luther's
Development," *Sixteenth Century Journal* 3 (1972): 50.

[21] LW 31:265–66, 266–67.

[22] LW 31:282.

[23] H. Schüssler, "Sacred Doctrine and the Authority of Scripture in
Canonistic Thought on the Eve of the Reformation," in *Reform and Authority
in the Medieval and Reformation Church*, ed. Guy F. Lytle (Washington, DC:
Catholic University of America Press, 1981), 62–64.

[24] LW 31:338.

arrived at his principle of authority before Leipzig.[25] Nevertheless, whenever this occurred, Luther not only rejected the view that the church preceded the Scripture but also dissolved the presumed marriage between the two. He had, by this point, arrived "at the irrefutable certainty that there is no 'prestabilized harmony' between Scripture and church, that Scripture exists prior to and is ranked before and above the church."[26]

Luther's reply from the pope ordered him to recant in sixty days or be excommunicated from the church. Convinced of the legitimacy of his convictions, Luther, during the morning of December 1520, stood just outside Wittenberg's east gate, with the university's faculty and students as witnesses to his public response. A bonfire was lit, and a host of papal books were symbolically tossed into the flames. Toward the end, Luther pulled the Bull of excommunication out of his academic gown and threw it into the fire as well, together with a copy of the canon law.

The divorce was official. Luther explained his case in *Why the Books of the Pope and His Disciples Were Burned*. The papacy, he argued, had set itself over God's word in such a way as to be above reproof. If the papacy's authority was legitimate, "they would gladly permit themselves to be examined and tried.... But," Luther continued, "the pope wants to blind everyone's eyes, let no one judge, but alone judge everyone."[27] This was demonstrable "by the fact," Luther declared, "that the pope has never once refuted with Scripture or reason anyone who has spoken, written, or acted against him, but has at all times suppressed, exiled, burned, or otherwise strangled him with force and bans."[28]

Knowing the fate he could meet (but providentially never did)—execution as a heretic—Luther continued to assert his position publicly. In the preface to *Defense and Explanation of All the*

---

[25] Bernard Lohse argues that even though Luther had not expressly stated his principle of Scripture alone by the time of his meeting with Cajetan in 1518, he was in fact working from it. See Lohse, "Luther und die Autorität Roms im Jahre 1518," in *Christian Authority*, ed. G.R. Evans (Oxford: Clarendon Press, 1988), 152.

[26] Lohse, *Martin Luther's Theology*, 188.

[27] LW 31:395.

[28] LW 31:395.

Articles, for example, he unequivocally stated his principle of authority and what became the formal principle of the so-called conservative Reformation:[29] "Scripture alone is the true lord and master of all
writings and doctrine on earth."[30] This "forever established the *Sola
Scriptura*"[31] for all to hear before the Imperial Diet at Worms (April
18, 1521), when he took his famous stand: "Unless I am convinced
by the testimony of the Scriptures or by clear reason (for I do not
trust either in the pope or in councils alone, since it is well known
that they have often erred and contradicted themselves), I am bound
by the Scriptures I have quoted and my conscience is captive to the
Word of God."[32]

Luther had essentially, albeit amid very different circumstances,
come to the principle of authority held by Irenaeus and the early
church fathers. And this cleared the way—by removing the theological innovations of the medieval centuries—for what Luther called a
"reformation according to holy Scripture."[33]

It is important to note that Luther (and the other magisterial reformers) did not conceive of or carry out this reformation as
theological revisionists. The Protestant doctrine of *sola Scriptura*
should not be understood as the rejection of church tradition in
favor of subjective and novel interpretations of the Bible. The
Lutheran reformers knew the dire consequences of Scripture being
interpreted in a vacuum; such an approach was already surfacing
amid the Anabaptists and left-wing radicals in the early days of the
Reformation. "We do not act as fanatically as the sectarian spirits
[i.e., Anabaptists]. We do not reject everything that is under the
dominion of the Pope," wrote Luther in 1528—even though his
excommunication was now a settled fact. He knew that the basic
creedal formulations of the church (the doctrine of the Trinity, the
deity of Christ, etc.) were still confessed by the Church of Rome.
Indeed, Luther conceded that it was from the papacy such sound

---

[29] This is the title of C. P. Krauth's magisterial treatise, *The Conservative
Reformation and Its Theology* (St. Louis, MO: Concordia Publishing House,
2007).

[30] LW 32:11–12.

[31] M. Reu, *Luther and the Scriptures* (Columbus: Wartburg Press, 1944), 19.

[32] LW 32:112.

[33] LW 32:122–23.

doctrine "descended to us."[34] What the conservative Reformers meant by *sola Scriptura*, then, should be understood as "Scripture... is the only inspired, infallible, final, and authoritative norm of faith and practice. It is to be interpreted in and by the church; and it is to be interpreted within the hermeneutical context of the rule of faith."[35] In other words, while the Bible is the only inspired word of God and the church and its traditions do not constitute a second, parallel source of revelation, the traditions of the Christian church can aid and temper the potential subjectivism and possible sectarianism of the scriptural interpreter. The fundamental imperative, however, is that all theological declarations should correspond to and be constrained by the word of God.

It was the Anabaptists and the broader radical reformers who took the doctrine of *sola Scriptura* to the extreme when they rejected traditional, historical interpretations of Scripture and preferred hermeneutical novelty instead. When it came to authority, they placed "the private judgment of the individual above the corporate judgment of the Christian Church concerning the interpretation of the Scripture."[36] And owing to their disdain for the historical church, many of them would effectively go their own way, situating themselves outside the boundaries of the church catholic.

To be sure, Rome would use such radicalism as positive proof of the heterodox nature of even the conservative Reformation. At the fourth session of the Council of Trent (1545–63), Rome accused Lutherans of "twisting the Scriptures" by subjecting the interpretation of the Bible to private judgment. In reality, all the Lutheran Reformation had done was to remove what the medieval church had *added* theologically and ecclesiastically in contradiction to biblical teaching. So in his *Examination of the Council of Trent*, the great Lutheran theologian Martin Chemnitz (1522–86) acknowledged the necessity of tradition as a check against innovative and subjective readings of the Bible manifest among the radical reformers and, at

---

[34] Oberman, "*Quo Vadis Petre?*," 285.

[35] Keith A. Mathison, "Solo Scriptura: The Difference a Vowel Makes," *Modern Reformation* 16/2 (2007): 26.

[36] Alister McGrath, *Reformation Thought: An Introduction* (Oxford: Basil Blackwell, 1988), 107.

the same time, disavowed the authority of the medieval papacy as an authority over Scripture:

> No one should rely on his own wisdom in the interpretation of the Scripture, not even in the clear passages, for it is clearly written in 2 Peter 1:20: "The Scripture is not a matter of one's private interpretation." And whoever twists the Holy Scripture so that it is understood according to his preconceived opinions does this to his own destruction (2 Peter 3:16). The best reader of the Scripture according to Hilary [of Poitiers, 300–368], is one who does not carry the understanding of what is said to the Scripture but who carries it away from the Scripture. We also gratefully and reverently use the labors of the fathers who by their commentaries have profitably clarified many passages of the Scripture. And we confess that we are greatly confirmed by the testimonies of the ancient church in the true and sound understanding of the Scripture. Nor do we approve of it if someone invents for himself a meaning which conflicts with all antiquity, and for which there are clearly no testimonies of the church.[37]

Here we have one of the clearest illustrations of the difference between the Lutheran and Roman principles of authority. Both respect traditional interpretations of the Scripture as a check against unwarranted innovation and radical theological revisionism. But for Lutherans, Scripture is the *sole* source of revelation and the *final* authority—whereas for Rome, Scripture, though certainly *an* authority owing to its revelatory character, is subject to tradition, particularly papal tradition, for its proper understanding and interpretation. This means in practice that tradition—an extrabiblical source of doctrine—is elevated to revelational status. Heiko Oberman described the official position of Rome this way: "The Council of Trent admits that not all doctrinal truths are to be found in Holy Scripture. Tradition is seen as a second doctrinal source which does not 'simply' unfold the content of Scripture…but adding its own substance complements Holy Scripture content-wise."[38]

---

[37] Martin Chemnitz, *The Examination of the Council of Trent*, trans. Fred Kramer (St. Louis, MO: Concordia Publishing House, 1971), 1:208–9.
[38] Oberman, "*Quo Vadis Petre?*," 288.

It is important to note that not just the Lutherans but also the Calvinists held the position that the Bible alone is God's word and that it should be normatively interpreted within the creedal context of the historic church. Calvin's *Institutes* asserts, "We willingly embrace and reverence as holy the early councils, such as Nicaea, Constantinople, Ephesus I, Chalcedon, and the like, which were concerned with refuting errors—in so far as they relate to the teaching of faith. For they contain nothing but the pure and genuine exposition of the Scripture, which the holy fathers applied with spiritual prudence to crush the enemies of religion."[39]

Where the Lutheran and Reformed disagreed was not so much in their principle of authority but in what they viewed as having priority in the systematic ordering of theology (for the Calvinists: the sovereignty of God; for Lutherans: the Incarnation and the Cross) and to what extent rational argument should inform biblical exegesis (e.g., in the understanding of the Lord's Supper—for the Lutherans: the real presence of the whole Christ, body and spirit, on the straightforward basis of Christ's declaration, "This is my body"; for the Calvinists: his spiritual presence only, since it would allegedly be irrational for Christ's body to be present other than at the right hand of God in heaven).

In the centuries that followed the Protestant Reformation, the viewpoint of the left-wing radicals that Scripture should be interpreted apart from any tradition began to coalesce into something new. During the eighteenth century, across the Atlantic in North America, the subjective and individualist interpretation of the radicals fused with Enlightenment rationalism and American populism. Keith Mathison has termed such a view of authority *solo Scriptura* ("Scripture interpreted by and for me alone")—in contradistinction to the Reformation doctrine of *sola Scriptura* ("Scripture alone").

This philosophy was rejected by the conservative Reformation, and for good reason. For while radical reformers claimed the authority of the Bible, epistemological priority (particularly when it came to interpreting the Bible) was ultimately given not to the church, as in the case of Rome, or to the Scripture itself, as with the Lutheran Reformation, but to the individual reader of the Scriptures. Thomas

---

[39] Quoted in Mathison, "Solo Scriptura," 27.

Müntzer (1488–1525), who was in many ways the *magister* of the radical reformers,[40] taught that God revealed himself directly to human beings. The illumination of the spirit then dictated how one interpreted the Bible.

It is not difficult to see how this approach in principle legitimizes any and every interpretation of the Bible. What eventually happened was a re-envisioning of historic Christianity, beginning in the sixteenth century and extending to the present day. Such an approach, stemming from unverifiable illuminations of "the spirit," was manifested by restorationists like Alexander Campbell (1788–1866), when he wrote, "I have endeavored to read the Scriptures as though no one had read them before."[41]

The consequence was and has been a proliferation of new Christian sects and heresies and eventually the nondenominational movement. Aaron B. Grosh (1800–1884), for example, could promote Universalism while calling the Bible the "one Master" that was his "only acknowledged creed book"—or Charles Beecher (1815–1900) could, on one hand, locate theological authority in the "Bible, the whole Bible, and nothing but the Bible" but, on the other hand, preach such novelties as the preexistence of the human soul before conception.[42]

As we said at the outset, the Christian church—even defined very broadly—has always recognized the authority of the Bible in one way or another. And for the most part, Christians—even nominal ones—place it at the center of their overall understanding of authority. For the Roman Catholic Church, the Scriptures are treated as God's revealed word but a word that is not really complete; God's revelation needs the completion offered by the traditions and interpretation of the church. Ecclesiastical traditions are viewed by Rome as a second—not secondary—source of revelation that not only adds to the biblical word of God but also determines how the Scriptures are to be understood.

---

[40] See Steven Ozment, *Mysticism and Dissent: Religious Ideology and Social Protest in the Sixteenth Century* (New Haven: Yale University Press, 1973), 61–97.

[41] Quoted in Mathison, "Solo Scriptura," 27.

[42] Mathison, "Solo Scriptura," 27.

Tradition, in this view, can confirm and perpetuate biblical doctrine, but it can also add elements not found in the text of the Bible. It can even, as in the case of dogmas such as the existence of purgatory or the perpetual virginity of Mary, squeeze beliefs out of the Bible that are quite foreign to a historical and grammatical analysis of its text. The same phenomenon may likewise be observed in Eastern Orthodox theology and even in the Anglican tradition.

Since the Reformation, Protestants of every stripe have reacted to this dual-source theory of authority. The most popular failing has been the initial elevation of the Bible above Christian tradition but then effectively jettisoning all or most all creedal and traditional ecclesiology, even when nowhere condemned by Scripture. This has left the church with a Bible in isolation from the history of Christianity; from reliable, classical biblical interpretation; and from the ecumenical creeds and the historic confessions. The result: a Bible that could be interpreted in almost any imaginable way, depending on the disposition, context, and predilections—linguistic and theological—of the interpreter. This approach can produce anything: the mystical and spiritualist type of Christianity first espoused by Thomas Müntzer in the sixteenth century, the premillennial dispensationalism of the Dallas Seminary and local church movement, or even the Muslim theology of the author of *The Bible Led Me to Islam*.

For all intents and purposes, *solo* (not *sola*) *Scriptura* is modern evangelicalism's view of authority. And a cursory survey of the broad spectrum of evangelicalism reveals that, while everyone claims to work from the same text, contradictory conclusions are the order of the day. The reason for this is that it is practically impossible to interpret the Bible objectively by a myopic look at the text as such. Interpreters of the Bible working from the principle of *solo Scriptura* may not interpret the Bible through the lens of unfortunate theological traditions, but they do interpret the Bible in accordance with their own biases. These biases can derive from contemporary culture, ideological assumptions, or anything that colors their worldview. Ultimately, what *solo Scriptura* does is to replace external tradition as a parallel source of theology alongside the Bible with a source that is internal, located within the *persona* of the interpreter.

The principle of *sola Scriptura* established by Luther not only militates against the dual-source theory of authority but, at the same time, mediates between it and the subjectivity of the *solo Scriptura* approach. On the one hand, any arbitrary elevation of episcopal tradition as a source of God's word and the consequent adding to the text of the Bible is rejected. On the other hand, there is the clear recognition that, while God's word is located in the Bible alone, it is necessarily received and interpreted by the historic church.

That church, however, being comprised of sinful people, is fallible. It is in need of continual reformation (*Ecclesia semper reformanda est*). To bring the church's theology back into line with God's word, Luther rightly saw the Scripture and the Scripture alone as the only instrument capable of achieving the needed corrections.

The Lutheran theological tradition sees itself not as an innovation of the sixteenth century but as the continuation of the church of Christ, founded on the apostles' teaching and preserved in spite of the corruptions of medieval and modern antibiblical doctrines and practices.

What *sola Scriptura* provides is a clear principle of authority for faith. To keep such faith grounded and constrained by the word of God, Lutherans are willing to listen to the history of the church. This does not mean naïvely accepting its errors; it means critiquing it where it has failed but at the same time accepting its gifts where they are consonant with biblical teaching.

Thus, the Lutheran Church is a confessional body—accepting with joy the ecumenical creeds of Christendom (the Apostles', Nicene, and Athanasian Creeds) and the magnificent confessional statements of the Reformation as contained in the *Book of Concord*. The contributions of the historic church are received with joy—but (to cite the Preface of the Formula of Concord, the last of those great Confessions) Scripture remains as the only standard by which all teachers and writings must be judged. For this reason, the Lutheran tradition offers Christians who strive to be faithful to God's word the surest way to order both their theology and their ecclesiastical and personal lifestyle.

Word of God in Islam and Christianity

Western philosophy, particularly in the realm of epistemology, has in many ways maintained that, to have certain knowledge about metaphysical things, such information would have to come from outside human experience and originate with God. This was expressed as far back as the time of Plato when he took up the issue of the nature and destiny of the human soul. In *Phaedo* he suggested that the only way to obtain certainty on such a matter was if there was a word from God (*logou theou*).[1] He assumed there wasn't one and so explained that man is left on his own to come up with the most plausible theory about the way things are. Some 2400 years later, Ludwig Wittgenstein expressed a similar position in his celebrated *Tractatus Logico-Philosophicus*. The perceived world is, as far as we know, all that is. Metaphysical propositions on the value and essence of things, if there are any, must come from outside of the world. But because "God does not reveal himself *in* the world," one "must pass over in silence" such matters.[2] In many ways, Wittgenstein set the tone for English and American philosophy for much of the twentieth century. Metaphysics and God-talk was considered, as A.J. Ayer put it, nonsensical and fictitious, for while there may be various claims that God had revealed information about the world and the way things really are, no religion offered any sort of verifiable evidence for it.[3]

---

[1] See Plato, *Phaedo,* 85d.
[2] From D.F. Pears and B.F. McGuiness's translation of Ludwig Wittgenstein's *Tractatus Logico-Philosophicus* (New York: Routledge, 1961), 73-74.
[3] A.J. Ayer, *Language, Truth and Logic* (Garden City: Dover Publications, 1946), 44-45, 115.

This critique of religion and its theological claims largely holds true for most of the world's religions.[4] Many don't even pretend to be based on a verifiable historical revelation from God. The only meaning they carry is that which the believer assigns to it. They certainly are not factual or truthful in an objective sense, even if whole civilizations value them. Christianity and Islam are different. Both assert God has *in fact* spoken in real human history. Accordingly, his revelation to man is, at least in principle, verifiable and therefore open to historical investigation. Christianity and Islam are in this sense unique. For not only do they make certain claims about God, his disposition towards men and women, and so on, like other religions, but they do so in a way that is objectively meaningful. Ultimately, they assert that God's word, and the certainty that comes with it, was and is in a factual sense available to human beings who, by virtue of their epistemic limits in reference to absolute truths, are stuck in a world of uncertainty. Both religions, then, must be taken seriously by anyone claiming to be interested in truth.

Both Christianity and Islam claim that God began to speak to man shortly after the creation of the first human. In Christianity, God's word to Adam began with almost unlimited blessings and a simple command not to eat the fruit of a certain tree in the midst of the garden. Then tragedy struck. Adam and Eve were seduced into disobeying God's command and, through them, "sin came into the world...and death through sin" (Rom. 5:12). This local sin had far-reaching consequences, Christianity claims, such that it affected the entire human race, condemning all as sinners before God in need of reconciliation but, due to this inherited sinful condition, without a way to achieve it on their own.

That is not the end of the story, though. In fact, in many ways it is just the beginning in Christianity. Seeing what Adam and Eve had done, God spoke yet again. This time, he condemned Adam and Eve for their sin, all the while making a promise that one day sin, death, and the devil would be crushed by an offspring descending from Eve.

---

[4] One may try to get around verificationism and its criticism of religion by appealing to various streams of postmodern thought. Such maneuvering, however, "places one in tension with the enterprise of serious inquiry." See C.J. Misak, *Verificationism: Its History and Prospects* (New York: Routledge, 1995).

Christianity has historically asserted that this first annunciation of the good news was passed down through the patriarchs and continually revealed through the prophets of old. Those who looked forward to the coming of this chosen offspring, because they ultimately trusted in the redeeming work of this forthcoming prophet (Deut. 18:15), priest (Gen. 14:18-20), and king (2 Sam. 7:12-16), were, as Eusebius put it, "Christians in fact if not in name."[5]

The word of God revealed to and through the various prophets of old, Christianity teaches, found its historical terminus in the person of Jesus Christ. He came not only claiming to be of God but provided evidence of it, such that when he, for example, fed the roughly five thousand men at Galilee, they responded by proclaiming, "This is indeed the prophet who is to come into the world" (John 6:14). But Jesus is not just seen as the last of a long series of prophets whose divinely inspired utterances were eventually recorded and regarded as holy writ. He is seen as the fulfillment of historical prophetic message and, moreover, incarnation of the very substantial word of God.

The ancient pedigree and theological continuity of the good news first iterated in the garden and fulfilled in Jesus was the earliest apologetic for the Christian faith. You see it already in Luke's Acts of the Apostles where Peter and Paul attempted to prove and persuade (e.g. 17:1-15; 26:24-29) those they spoke to from the Hebrew Bible that Jesus was the one whom God had promised, as "all the prophets" had borne witness (10:43). It was developed by the early apologists and became part of the classical Christian view of history particularly in its apologetic contest with Judaism.

But then came Islam, and it challenged all this by rewriting history. Its narrative of God's word transmitted in history begins in a similar manner. As in Christianity, Adam is regarded as the first human being as well as the first recipient of God's revelation. The circumstances in which God spoke to him are, however, very different. The Qur'an teaches that Adam and Eve were originally placed in a garden located in the heavens. They were commanded to refrain from eating the fruit from a particular tree within it but disobeyed. They

---

[5] Eusebius, *The History of the Church*, trans. G.A. Williamson (New York: Penguin Books, 1965), I.4.6.

were subsequently cast out and made to fall to the earth, whereupon
they were forgiven, and Adam was made the first prophet of God
when God, as Qur'an 2:37 puts it, "gave him words."

The words that were given to Adam were qualitatively different than what one finds in Genesis, and mark one of the significant
theological differences between the two religions, for they were not
words of promise but rather words of what the Qur'an calls guidance
(*huda*). According to Islamic theology, God began with Adam to
provide specific instructions on what to believe and how to live. So
long as Adam and his descendants obeyed them, their relationship
with God and their fellow man would be one of peacefulness or *salām*,
but God also tells Adam in Qur'an 2:38-39 that "those who disbelieve
and deny our messages shall be the inhabitants of the fire, and there
they will remain."

Here begins the lineage of the prophets in Islamic thought.
Parallel yet contrary to Christianity's view of the continuity of the
promise of God being delivered through prophets, Islam sees God's
perpetually transmitted word as essentially ethical guidance. It begins
with Adam and was continuously delivered by a great many prophets up to the time of Muhammad. Some of them—normally desig-
nated as messengers or apostles—even produced books: Moses, the
Torah; David, the Psalms; and Jesus, the *Injil* or Gospel. Along with
the twenty or more prophets named in the Qur'an and thousands of
unnamed others, they all taught submission to and peace with God
by following his guidance.

In other words, Adam, Noah, Abraham, Moses, David, Jesus,
and countless others are seen by Muslims as prophets of Islam. And
they all, beginning with Adam, saw the deliverance of the word of God
as terminating with Muhammad. As one tradition reads,

> When Adam committed sin he said: "O Lord, I ask you by the right
> of Muhammad, will you forgive me?" God said: "How do you know
> about Muhammad, I have not yet created him?" Adam said: "Lord,
> because when you created me with your hand and breathed into me
> from your spirit, I raised my head and saw what was written on the
> foundations of your throne: There is no god but God and Muhammad
> is the Apostle of God. I knew that you would not place his name there
> unless he is the most beloved of creation to you." God said: "You are

right, Adam. He is the most beloved of creation to me. When you ask me in the right of his name, I will forgive you. If only for Muhammad did I create you.[6]

According to Qur'an 61:6, even Jesus looked forward to the coming of Muhammad when he announced the "good news" of a messenger coming after him named Ahmed as name for Muhammad (elsewhere Ahmad).

Islam sees Muhammad—and, more importantly, the revelation delivered through him—as the end of the prophetic lineage, as well as the perfection of God's guidance. The famous Indian Islamic revivalist Abu 'l-A'la Mawdudi summarized this point well when he wrote, "God's true Prophets were raised in all countries: in every land and people. They all possessed one and the same religion—the religion of Islam. No doubt, the methods of teaching and the legal codes…were a little different in accordance with the needs of and the stage of culture of the people among whom they were raised."[7] God universalized his law, however, by the end of Muhammad's ministry when he declared through Muhammad the perfection of what he had progressively revealed through the ages (Qur'an 5:3). God's word to humankind was now a "complete and full-fledged system, covering all aspects of individual and material life of man. [Muhammad] was made a Prophet for the entire human race and was deputed to propagate his mission to the whole world."[8]

The conviction of the truthfulness of this alternative—Islamic—history of the transmission of God's word gave way to Muslim polemics and apologetics vis-à-vis Christianity. You see it already in the Qur'an at 3:64ff where Muhammad calls Christians to a common—presumably monotheistic—platform only to inform them that, while they may claim to fall in line with the faith of Abraham (and Adam before him), the real faith passed down through the ages was Islam. In light or in anticipation of counter arguments based on the lack of textual support from Moses' Torah, David's Psalms, or the Gospel of

---

[6] Brannon M. Wheeler, *Prophets in the Quran: An Introduction to the Quran and Muslim Exegesis* (New York: Continuum Books, 2002), 30.

[7] Abu 'l-A'la Mawdudi, *Towards Understanding Islam*, 22nd edn. (Lahore: Idara Tarjuman-ul-Quran, 1995), 43.

[8] Mawdudi, 48.

Jesus that such a continuity exists, these assertions were backed up by Muslim apologists' claims that Christians misinterpreted earlier prophetic books, forcing its words into a procrustean bed of Christian theology. If only the right hermeneutic was employed—the quranic hermeneutic—then one would see the continuity between biblical and quranic teaching. Later, though, this morphed into the charge that the text itself had been altered by copyists to support a theology that developed out of the fusion of Greco-Roman ideas and the Jewish religion. This is the position most Muslim approaches to Christianity employ today, and they now take the work of text critics like Bart Ehrman as their ally in asserting such things like the British Muslim Louay Fatoohi's claim that much of what one finds in the gospels, especially the high Christology of all of them, "were never part of the Injīl [Gospel] and were added by their respective authors and editors."[9]

The conflicting and irreconcilable claims each tradition makes concerning the word of God did not keep Christians and Muslims from investigating the position of the other. There is, in fact, a long tradition of Christian theological discourse on Islam that began around the mid-eighth century, just a few generations after the conquest and subjugation of Byzantine Christian populations under Islamic rule. Much of it was comparative, for didactic purposes, but there was almost always an accompanying polemic or apologetic component. What is perhaps most interesting for our present topic is that, rather than simply assuming the superiority of the Bible and Christian exegesis of it followed by the denouncement of Islam and limiting the discussion there, many early Christian authors on Islam went further and attempted to demonstrate the theological superiority of Christianity. Some even hoped to persuade Muslims to embrace Christianity. And they did so not so much by focusing on the inscripturation of the word of God, for they knew that the Muslim assumption that the Qur'an was God's word was—as basic presuppositions are—practically impenetrable. So, they sought to demonstrate the truthfulness of the incarnation of the word of God, and they did so, in part, on the basis of the Qur'an.

---

[9] Louay Fatoohi, *Mystery of the Historical Jesus* (Birmingham, UK: Safis Publishing, 2007), 37-38.

It began with John of Damascus (c. 676-749).[10] In his work *On Heresies* (part two of a larger work entitled *Fountain of Knowledge*), he provided a brief explanation of the Qur'an's origins and an outline of Islamic theology. Almost immediately, he drew attention to the Qur'an's reference to Christ as the "word of God" (*kalimatullah;* 4:171) but, at the same time, its insistence that he was also a creature of God created by God's command in the womb of Mary (3:47). He sheds more light on the issue in his "manual of guidance for Christians who find themselves entering into theological discussions with Muslims" entitled *The Discussion of a Christian and a Saracen* (Saracen is a medieval term for Muslim).[11] "If you are asked by a Saracen: 'What do you call Christ?'" John wrote, "say to him, 'The Word of God.'"[12] And be confident, for this is what the Scriptures call him. Moreover, this—the *kalimatullah*—is what the Qur'an calls him.

John also knew that the Muslim theological tradition had developed a theology of the word of God being eternal or uncreated. It, however, limited the temporal manifestation of God's word to the text of the Qur'an. In doing so, though, it limited God—mutilated him, as he put it in *On Heresies*—from manifesting himself differently in, for example, a person like Jesus Christ. In other words, while Islam permitted the inscripturation of God's word, it arbitrarily precluded an incarnation, even though at least in one place—in the Qur'an—it acknowledges it, at least according to John's exegesis. This should come as no surprise, though, for Islam and the Qur'an was, according to John of Damascus, an incoherent assimilation of Christian scriptural traditions (and others) under the influence of an Arian monk.[13]

Unlike their Eastern counterparts, Christians in the West were mostly isolated from Islam for most of its early medieval development

---

[10] See Daniel J. Sahas, *John of Damascus on Islam* (New York: E.J. Brill, 1972).

[11] Hugh Goddard, *A History of Christian-Muslim Relations* (New York: New Amsterdam Books, 2000), 40-41.

[12] John of Damascus, *The Discussion of a Christian and a Saracen,* in *The Early Christian-Muslim Dialogue: A Collection of Documents from the First Three Centuries (632-900 A.D.),* ed. N.A. Newman (Sheffield: Interdisciplinary Biblical Research Institute, 1993), 144-147.

[13] John of Damascus, *On Heresies,* in *The Early Christian-Muslim Dialogue,* 139-141.

(except those in Spain). But at the beginning of the High Middle Ages they, too, began to develop polemics against it. It started with Abbot Peter of Cluny (c. 1092-1156), when he began thinking about the opportunity of evangelistic work amidst Muslims during the early crusades in the Levant.[14] And in many ways he set in motion the medieval European dream of converting Muslims to Christianity by sponsoring the translation of the Qur'an as well as other Muslim literature around the early 1140s so that the theological study of Islam could be facilitated. Not much more was accomplished, though, as the Muslim counterattack on the crusaders and their recently acquired kingdoms in the Near East, beginning with Salah al-Din's conquest of Jerusalem, began. The missionary vision to convert Muslims started to be realized again at the end of the thirteenth century, particularly with the establishment of the Franciscan and Dominican mendicant orders. But whereas the Franciscans focused on what might be described as works of mercy when living amongst Muslims, the Dominicans developed a theological approach.[15] Much of it was inspired in methodology by Thomas Aquinas' great *Summa contra Gentiles* but soon became much more specialized and directed not at some abstract gentile but at the Saracens.

The most influential among the Dominican Islamic specialists was the Italian missionary to Baghdad named Riccoldo da Monte di Croce (c. 1240-1320).[16] He spent a number of years in the 1290s in and around Baghdad amidst Muslim scholars until he was recalled back to Italy at the turn of the century. It was here that he penned his famous and influential *Contra legem Saracenorum* wherein, after fourteen chapters of polemical tearing down of the Qur'an, he tried to demonstrate the truthfulness of Christianity from its text. His hope

---

[14] See James Kritzeck, *Peter the Venerable and Islam* (Princeton: Princeton University Press, 1964).

[15] See J. Hoeberichts, *Francis and Islam* (St. Bonaventure, NY: Franciscan Institute Publications, 1997) and John Victor Tolan, *Saracens: Islam in the Medieval Imagination* (New York: Columbia University Press, 2002), 233-255.

[16] See L. Michael Spath, "Riccoldo da Monte Croce: Medieval Pilgrim and Traveler to the Heart of Islam," *Bulletin of the Royal Institute for Inter-Faith Studies* 1:1 (1999): 55-102; "*De Lege Sarracenorum* According to Riccoldo da Monte Croce," *Bulletin of the Royal Institute for Inter-Faith Studies* 2:2 (2000): 115-140.

was that Muslims hearing such arguments would be compelled by force of reason to believe them. Riccoldo did so by drawing Christian doctrines out of the Qur'an. A good Dominican, he did not take the Qur'an to be authoritative *per se*. In fact, he saw the Qur'an as a devious book filled with ancient heresies and an infinite number of lies. But, as a missionary, he knew that amidst Muslims, who in his experience were eager to hear about the particularities of Christian doctrine, he had to start somewhere. And since Muhammad and the compilers of the Qur'an were not the most scrupulous of editors when they fabricated the quranic text from, among others, Christian texts, they unwittingly left enough trace evidence of Christian doctrine in it that could be used to persuade Muslims of the veracity of God's triune nature, the deity of Christ, and the authority of the Bible.

His argument for Jesus as the word of God from all eternity is similar to that of John of Damascus. He starts with reference to Qur'an 3:45 and 4:171 and their "unequivocal" affirmation that "Christ is the word of God." This attribution is not used metaphorically nor is it a title for someone who speaks for God, he argued, for no other prophet—in the Qur'an—is referred to as the word of God. It is used in reference to Christ as a real and uniquely personal attribution. And, he continues,

> [I]f the word is taken literally, it is clear that the word of God would be everlasting and true God. For just as the word that proceeds from the mouth of a perishable man is necessarily perishable, so the word that proceeds from the everlasting mouth, through which He made the heaven and earth and the things that are in between (as the Koran likes to say) is necessarily everlasting and imperishable. Moreover, whatever proceeds from God is essentially God and in this way the word of God is God.... Therefore, Mohammed spoke the truth when he said that Jesus Christ the son of Mary is also the word of God.[17]

He just didn't understand what he was doing. Interestingly, while Riccoldo suggests this was simply due to his ignorance of what he copied from Christian sources, Luther suggested in his German

---

[17] Riccoldo da Monte di Croce, *Refutation of the Koran*, trans. Londini Ensis (Charleston: Self-Published, 2010), 85-88.

translation of Riccoldo's work that the Holy Spirit caused such things to be written in the Qur'an.[18]

These arguments, particularly in the initial stages of Christian and Muslim theological interaction, may have gained some traction in the Muslim world. For example, the first orthodox Christian that we know of to write primarily in Arabic, Theodor Abu Qurra (c. 750-829), is recorded in a few Christian and Muslim sources to have publically debated Muslim scholars at the invitation of the caliph al-Ma'mun (813-833), in what seems to have been a remarkably liberal environment. And it was here that an agreement was reached between Christian and Muslim participants that Jesus was in fact "the word of God." This was followed by disagreement over whether he was the uncreated (i.e., divine) word of God or the word of God in the sense that he was created in the womb of Mary when God spoke him into existence by simply saying, "Be."[19]

This is the quranic position (3:47, 59). And Muslim responses to the particular argument for Christ as the "word of God" quickly developed in light of it. In the ninth century, perhaps in response to the perceived headway or theological concessions Christian apologists achieved,[20] as Christians were reduced to the status of second-class citizens by the caliph al-Mutawakkil (847-861), the orthodox Islamic position on the identity of the word of God was definitively established. Two major figures associated with this are Ahmad ibn Hanbal (d. 855) and Abu al-Hasan al-Ash'ari (d. 935). Both argued and established the position that, while God's word was eternal and uncreated, its temporal manifestation was only located in the text of the Qur'an.[21]

---

[18] *Luthers Werke: Kritische Gesamtausgabe* (Weimar: H.Böhlau, 1883–2009), 53:366 [Hereafter WA]: "Also hat in der heilige Geist vermanet und getrieben, das er hat muessen mit worten unsers Glaubens hoechsten Artickel aussprechen."

[19] See Goddard, 53; Alfred Guillaume, "Theodore Abu Qurra as Apologist," *Muslim World* 15 (1925):42-51. Cf with the critical commentary of John C. Lamoreaux, *Theodore Abu Qurrah* (Provo: Brigham Young University Press, 2005), xvii-xviii.

[20] Goddard, 41; Morris S. Seale, *Muslim Theology: A Study of Origins with Reference to the Church Fathers* (London: Luzac & Co., 1964).

[21] See http://www.yale.edu/faith/downloads/rp/WordGodIslamChristianity-English.pdf.

The Qur'an is, in other words, God's word inscripturated. But it has not become incarnated.

Herein lies the essential theological divide between Christianity and Islam that has been debated for centuries since the initial medieval encounters between Christians and Muslims. And it is right that this issue has been front and center in historical Christian-Muslim discourse. What's interesting, though, is the way the issue of the word of God in Islam and Christianity is being treated today. Muslim theologians, for the most part, have stuck with their classical position. The Qur'an is the inscripturated word of God. It is therefore *al-Furqan* or the standard, which has been "sent down" from God (Qur'an 25:1), and by which all things should be judged. And so when they approach Christianity, it is interpreted and addressed through the lens of the Qur'an.

One of the more high-profile examples of this is the common word movement. It began in Fall of 2007, a year after the fallout from Pope Benedict's Regensburg lecture, when 138 representatives from across Islamic civilization gathered together and sent an open letter and call (*da'wa*) to the Pope and leaders of Christian churches every-where.[22] In short, it argued that, because Christians and Muslims comprise nearly half of the world's population, it behooves both to work towards a peaceful reconciliation of the two faiths. And in fact both can be reconciled, for each shares a tremendous amount of common ground found in each tradition's sacred text. The Christian response to this was (sadly) rather predictable. Immediately, hundreds of churchmen and scholars of every confession accepted the terms of what amounts to a veiled call to Islam.[23] Such is the character of much Christian consideration of Islam. At best, though, Christians nowadays tend to take the comparative approach—pitting one text and its teachings against the other—assuming they have God's word while Islam doesn't. And at worst, they take the approach of the late Wilfred Cantwell Smith and remain ambivalent to the whole question of epistemology and authority.[24]

---

[22] See http://www.acommonword.com/.

[23] Sam Solomon and E. Al Maqdisi, *A Common Word: The Undermining of the Church* (Afton, VA: Advancing Native Missions, ANM, 2009).

[24] Wilfred Cantwell Smith, "Is the Qur'an the Word of God?" in *On Understanding Islam* (Berlin: Mouton Publishers, 1981), 282-300.

There is a different approach, however. It has much in common with the initial attempts of Christians such as John of Damascus and Riccoldo da Monte di Croce in that it focuses on the issue of the word of God and Jesus. But its starting point is not the Qur'an. It is with history.

Both Christianity and Islam claim that God has spoken his word through certain prophets and in the texts that record their message throughout history. These texts (the Bible and the Qur'an) are respectively regarded as the word of God by each tradition. The texts and their teachings contradict each other on a number of points. Where they do agree is in their identification of Jesus as a prophet. Christianity goes further, of course, declaring Jesus was equally the incarnation of the prophetic word of God. It does so not as the result of the process of theological development, as Muslims allege, but on the basis of Jesus' own testimony about himself.

The big question between Christians and Muslims in the realm of epistemology is whether or not there is sufficient evidence to make this claim. To make a long apologetic story short, the answer is a resounding yes. The Gospels prove to be solid primary source material from which one can determine the nature of the life, work, and claims of Jesus (despite the claims of some of the higher critics masquerading as text critics and enthusiasts of the non-canonical gospels). In them, Jesus unmistakably associates himself with God yet also distinguishes himself from God the Father (John 20:17). John provides the explanation when he describes him as the *logos* of God. Jesus was (and is) the substantive word of God in time and space in a particular person.

Muslims claim essentially the same thing about the Qur'an. It is God's eternal speech inscribed in a text. When it is recited, it is as if God is speaking from all eternity. The problem is that there is no evidence that can be adduced to support this assertion. So, they argue that the Qur'an itself is evidence of its divine nature. It claims to be the word of God; therefore, it is the word of God. With Jesus, the circumstances are different. Christianity does not demand circular, fideistic reasoning to establish its legitimacy, for according to the apologetic tradition up to and through John Warwick Montgomery, there is ample evidence to trust Jesus was who he claimed to be. The resurrection is the best proof, so to speak, of it. It is even more far-reaching than that, though, argues Montgomery, as it "constitutes an event subject to investigation: its synthetic character removes the central Christian claim that 'God was in Christ, reconciling the world unto himself' from the realm of technical meaninglessness into which…so many religions fall."[25] This would, if no evidence can be adduced for its claims, include Islam. Montgomery goes further and argues that the resurrection not only validates Jesus' divinity but also, through inductive processes, can lead to the conclusion that the Hebrew Bible and the apostolic writings are God's inspired written word.[26] This goes a long way in establishing the truthfulness of the claim that "God spoke to our fathers by the prophets, but in these last days he has spoken to us by his Son" (Heb. 1:1-2), especially in a context where Islam and its claims to supremacy often escape the scrutiny of Christians. In a context such as ours, then, in the midst of a global resurgence of Islam, it's time that the facts be restored to our thinking and in our persuasive discourse with Muslims concerning the *verbum* that *caro factum est*, for the incarnation of the word of God did not happen in an epistemological corner (Acts 26:26).

---

[25] John Warwick Montgomery, *Tractatus Logico-Theologicus* (Bonn: VKW, 2002), 97.

[26] Montgomery, 129.

Positive Apologetics

Christian apologetics is generally defined as the defense of the faith. Some would characterize it as the exoneration of the faith against false caricatures. Others see it as a polemical endeavor; that is, the apologist is one who critiques and exposes the logical incoherence of non-Christian worldviews and religions. What is controversial relative to the nature of apologetics is whether or not it can be approached in a positive fashion, especially in service of evangelism. Such an approach usually begins by trying to persuade a non-Christian of: 1) the general historical reliability of the gospels; 2) Christ's deity (based on his miracles, especially the resurrection); and 3) the inspiration of the Scripture (on the basis of Jesus' own view of the Hebrew Bible and promise of the truthfulness of the testimony of the apostles [John 14-16], which would eventually comprise the New Testament).

For decades, John Warwick Montgomery has argued that there is certainly a place for this within the framework of classic Lutheran theology.[1] He has also consistently exposed the shallow rejections of it from works of prominent Lutheran theologians, noting that between both liberals and conservatives is a rejection of positive apologetics that "is virtually indistinguishable! Both claim that Christian revelation stands beyond proof and beyond demonstration—and that any attempt to offer an apologetic to establish its validity is to misunderstand the nature of the Christian gospel."[2] The case against apolo-

---

[1] See, among others, Montgomery, "Lutheranism and the Defense of the Faith," *The Lutheran Synod Quarterly* 11 (Fall 1970): 1-45; "The Incarnate Christ: The Apologetic Thrust of Lutheran Theology," *Modern Reformation* 7 (1998): 8-12.

[2] Montgomery, "Lutheranism and the Defense of the Faith," 15.

getics that might serve evangelism is not closed, however, for if "the Spirit works through the Word, and…the Word sets forth accurate historical knowledge of Christ's life and saving work," this does not "preclude the apologetic use of such evidence. Historical knowledge, like reason, can be misused by sinful man; but it—again like reason— can be brought into obedience to Christ and employed ministerially to persuade men to accept the historical Christ as Lord of their personal history."[3] The apologist uses reason in a ministerial fashion to point the unbeliever to the facts concerning the historical Jesus of the Bible. He seeks to persuade the unbeliever of who Jesus claimed to be and what he did. Such an approach attempts to generate *fides historica* or historical knowledge. It does not treat such *fides* or knowledge as saving faith, but does recognize, as does historic Lutheranism, that such knowledge (*notitia*) is the objective foundation of faith in terms of its assent (*assensus*) and ultimately trust (*fiducia*) in Christ alone.

One of the more significant critiques of this approach comes from the presuppositionalist school of apologetics. It claims that an inductive and evidential approach to apologetic evangelism is, at best, doomed to failure and, at worst, dangerously close to conceding too much to secular epistemologies inimical to the gospel. It is doomed to failure because, the presuppositionalist maintains, the total depravity of humankind has so far destroyed the cognition of men and women that even when faced with solid evidence and reasoned arguments, they will always interpret such data in light of their non-Christian worldview.

Worldviews are determinative, it is alleged; they are like a pair of mental glasses through which all facts are viewed and interpreted. As such, the presuppositionalist argues that "apologists…should legitimately require the unbeliever to reason on Christian presuppositions."[4] He cannot persuade inductively from reason. Unbelievers and their attendant worldviews are necessarily inimical to the gospel. To employ reasoning that they might accept is to concede to the legitimacy of the worldview with which it is associated. There is no

---

[3] Montgomery, "Christian Apologetics in the Light of the Lutheran Confessions," *Concordia Theological Quarterly* 42 (1978): 264.

[4] John Frame, "Presuppositional Apologetics," in *Five Views on Apologetics*, ed. Stanly N. Gundry (Grand Rapids: Zondervan, 2000), 218.

neutrality. To suggest there is willfully disobeys the call to bring every thought captive to the obedience of Christ.

This sort of epistemology leads to an apologetic whereby one assumes, and demands that the unbeliever assume, what the apologist attempts to demonstrate. Despite the obvious logical fallacy—the *petitio principii*—presuppositionalists demand such an approach. As a recently published apologetics textbook put it, the Christian answer to the unbeliever's inquiry into why one should believe the articles of the Christian faith to be true should be that "God says so. It is true because *God says so*. How do I know God says so? Because *he says he says so!*" One has to use the Bible to prove the truth of the Bible. "If the non-Christian insists that you cannot…you need to explain that you really would not be consistent if you allowed some other authority to become the rule by which you judge God's word."[5]

The issues raised over against positive apologetics revolve around the relationship between faith and reason or, more precisely, epistemology. Those who object to positive apologetics on the above grounds usually do so, it seems, because they do not (perhaps cannot) distinguish between epistemology and soteriology. This results in what is often termed fideism, an epistemology that is content with justifying or defending knowledge—at least certain fields of knowledge—by appealing only to faith. Alvin Plantinga describes it as an "exclusive or basic reliance upon faith alone, accompanied by a consequent disparagement of reason and utilized especially in the pursuit of philosophical or religious truth."[6]

Fideism is highly problematic. For one, it at least implicitly rejects the correspondence theory of truth, which says there is a real world of facts—present and historical—that exists outside of us, and that, in this real world, things are as they are regardless of whether we perceive or believe in them or not. Fideism pays no heed nor attempts to give any epistemic justification or apologetic (apart from the claim to faith) for why one holds something to be the case. When applied

---

[5] Richard B. Ramsay, *The Certainty of the Faith: Apologetics in an Uncertain World* (Phillipsburg, New Jersey: P&R Publishing, 2007), 150, 166.

[6] Alvin Plantinga, "Reason and Belief in God," in *Faith and Rationality: Reason and Belief in God*, eds. Alvin Plantinga and Nicholas Wolterstorff (South Bend: University of Notre Dame Press, 1983), 87.

to Christianity, it effectively reduces it to a cult of private belief and religious experience that stands on the same epistemological ground as all other religions.

There have always been fideists of some sort or another in the history of Christian thought. It became especially widespread in the period of late modernity when the church found itself incapable of standing up to the rising tide of naturalism. So it began to separate itself from the world. Soon, a sort of cognitively dissonant view of the world emerged that said there was a world of fact available and knowable to all regardless of religious disposition. Only off on the fringe, available only to the indoctrinated, existed a private world of values. Religion and its attendant historical narrative (such as the resurrection of Jesus) belonged "exclusively to the private world."[7] One could believe in such religious values if they wished, but it was, at best, an unknowable event and, at worst, tantamount to a superstitious belief. When this move was made and Christians began to concede to this split, the confession of classic creedal Christianity, which saw (and sees) the events of Jesus' life (even the miraculous events) as happening in real empirical history ("under Pontius Pilate"), increasingly found itself walled off from the world in a self-imposed confessional ghetto.

In many ways we are still there. A strong positive apologetic could work towards remedying this, but there is a lot of resistance towards it. It is especially seen in postmodern theologies that strive to justify the church's existence while at the same time dismissing apologetics. The arguments are multifaceted and appear in numerous publications. Perhaps the most focused (and earliest) was advanced by Philip Kenneson in *Christian Apologetics in the Postmodern World*. Contemporary Christians in postmodern times are, in his view, absolved of contending for the truthfulness of the Gospel. "Christians need not continue to answer 'the truth question,'" for truth is recognized as a relative term.[8] For Kenneson, what is regarded as true can only be true if it somehow connects (or is related) to a "web of

---

[7] Lesslie Newbigin, *The Foolishness to the Greeks: The Gospel and Western Culture* (Grand Rapids: Eerdmans, 1986), 49.

[8] Phillip Kenneson, "There's No Such Thing as Objective Truth, and It's a Good Thing," in *Christian Apologetics in the Postmodern World*, eds. Timothy Phillips and Dennis Okholm (Downers Grove: IVP, 1995), 161.

convictions, beliefs and practices" already in place that determines what is true or false, and not the other way around.

A positive, fact-based apologetic is ill-equipped to meet the postmodern challenges of the day. By beginning in alleged neutral territory (e.g., in the realm of history) with unbelief and, then, building a demonstrable case for the truthfulness of Christianity, one adopts "Enlightenment optimism about the role of...reason in the recognition of truth."[9] Truth—especially metaphysical or theological truth—really cannot be known. It can only be believed. Or, as James Smith boldy puts it, "We can't *know* that God was in Christ reconciling the world to himself. The best we can do is *believe*."[10] And all the church and Christians can or should do is proclaim its beliefs. Of course the church should proclaim the gospel. No one would dispute this. The problem is that it confuses apologetics with proclamation.

This isn't just Smith's postmodern position, though. It is also expressed in Pieper when he described the assertion, "The best apology of the Christian religion is its proclamation," as axiomatic.[11] This seems to be the position of much of confessional Lutheranism, too. All that is needed is the proclamation of law and gospel. "Unbelief," writes David Scaer, "is dissipated by the Gospel only after the Law has been preached." It is not "removed by the alleged attractive rationality of Christianity." While apologetics can be used in a negative fashion, to address those attempting to "destroy faith among believers or to hinder those who are approaching the church," it cannot be used positively or persuasively. To do so—that is, attempting to persuade others of the historical revelation of God in Christ—teeters on "the error of Rationalism."[12] But what if the preaching of Christianity which hinges on an historical person and event (see 1 Corinthians 15:1-19) is largely regarded as a culturally perpetuated

---

[9] James Smith, *Who's Afraid of Postmodernism?* (Grand Rapids: Baker, 2006), 28.

[10] Smith, *Who's Afraid of Postmodernism?* 119.

[11] Franz Pieper, *Christian Dogmatics*, (St. Louis, CPH, 1950), 1:109.

[12] David P. Scaer, "Apologetics as Theological Discipline: Reflections on a Necessary and Biblical Task," in *Let Christ be Christ: Theology, Ethics, & World Religions in the Two Kingdoms*, ed. Daniel N. Harmelink (Huntington Beach: Tentatio Press, 1999), 302.

myth or even the product of some ancient theological and political conspiracy? In other words, what if the historical events of the gospel—that Jesus died on a cross while Pontius Pilate was prefect of Judea and rose again from the dead three days later—are regarded as untrue? There's a whole host of material available for mass consumption and enjoyed by popular culture—from Dan Brown's conspiracy theories to new atheist literature to the popular works of Bart Ehrman, Elaine Pagels, et al.—that sanctions this. Add to this the influx of new and exotic world religions and their competing claims, naturalism and the ideology of scientism, as well as the relativism and agnosticism of postmodernism, all taking root in what many call the post-church culture of America, and, it seems, that the need for an apologetic that takes Christianity on the offense is obvious. To see ourselves as absolved of the apologetic task is suicidal. J.P. Moreland said it well:

> [P]ostmodernism is a form of intellectual pacifism that, at the end of the day, recommends backgammon while the barbarians are at the gate. It is the easy cowardly way out that removes the pressure to engage alternative conceptual schemes, to be different, to risk ridicule, to take a stand outside the gate. But it is precisely as disciples of Christ, even more, as officer in his army, that the pacifist way out is simply not an option. However comforting it may be, postmodernism is the cure that kills the patient, the military strategy that concedes defeat before the first shot is fired, the ideology that undermines its own claims to allegiance. And it is an immoral, coward's way out that is not worthy of a movement born out of the martyr's blood.[13]

The same goes for fideism, too. Though it is often dressed up in pious clichés, it is just as self-defeating as recent trends in postmodernism, for it leaves the church in a theological ghetto with words that ring hollow before the unbelieving world. None of this is to suggest that apologetics is a cure-all for evangelism. But for a world that largely and increasingly sees Christianity as a first-century myth perpetuated

---

[13] J.P. Moreland, "Postmodernism and Truth," in *Reasons for Faith: Making a Case for the Christian Faith,* ed. Norman L. Geisler and Chad V. Meister (Wheaton: Crossway Books, 2007), 126.

by the remnant of traditional Western culture, apologetics works towards demonstrating that what we confess is not a cleverly or culturally disguised myth, but it is in fact what God himself did in real historical time and space for us and for the world. In short, along with preaching and everything else the church does, apologetics works to advance the gospel.

Luther's Use of Apologetics

The title of this paper may seem strange, for every good Lutheran knows that Luther considered reason deceitful and even dangerous to faith and theology (reason is, after all, "the Devil's whore"). Apologetics employs reason to defend and even demonstrate the objectivity of the faith. Therefore, Luther was and would be opposed to any sort of fact-based and rational apologetic.

This is, of course, a caricature of those among us that are skeptical of apologetics. No one has ever published such an argument. But spend enough time in the discipline of apologetics and you will find your confessional friends distancing themselves from you for your "rationalism." Your pietist friends will begin to express concern for your lack of spirituality. And the liberal acquaintances you keep (assuming they could tolerate having a friend like you in the first place) will chuckle at your naïve belief that something like objective truth exists in the first place.

The concern and even disdain some have for apologetics may be, in part, due to the apologist him- or herself. Apologists (like some theologians) can be overbearing, obsessive, and arrogant as they pursue Peter's exhortation to always be prepared to make a defense for the hope that we have in Christ but ignore the instruction to do it with gentleness and respect. More common, however, is the objection coming from a culture of anti-intellectualism and/or a confusion of soteriology with epistemology manifesting itself in a type of fideism. Nevertheless, apologetics remains what David Scaer once described as a biblical and necessary task.[1]

---

[1] See David Scaer, "Apologetics as Theological Discipline: Reflections on a Necessary and Biblical Task," in *Let Christ be Christ: Theology, Ethics & World*

The church has always provided an apologetic witness to the faith. The gospels were written so that one could know and that its readers would be "persuade[d]...that Jesus is the Christ, God's Son, who came to save sinners."[2] Paul customarily reasoned with Jews in their synagogues, argued for the truthfulness of the faith before babbling philosophers, and tried to persuade the authorities that Jesus rose from the dead, not in some meta-historical corner but as a matter of historical fact. When and where the gospel sounded like superstitious nonsense, the earliest Christians argued to the contrary; it was (and is) not a cleverly devised myth but a confession of what God had done in time and space, as so many eyewitnesses had borne witness. And as resistance to Christianity increased, geographically and intellectually, apologists from Justin Martyr to Augustine persisted in their defense of and arguments for its truthfulness.

Even after the Christianization of Europe in the Middle Ages, the need remained for answers to Jewish objections. An even greater challenge emerged with the geographical extension and belligerence of Islam. In the midst of the Crusades, Christians learned that, unlike the Jews and the Old Testament, they had little to no common ground to reason with Muslims. So, after translating and studying the Qur'an and other Islamic source material, they began to fashion polemics and new apologetic strategies for Muslims in Spain and wherever missionaries accompanying Crusaders might encounter them. It was probably the Muslims in Spain, and not merely some abstract audience of theologians, that Anselm had in my mind when he penned his *Cur Deus Homo* before the turn of the eleventh century.

The high Middle Ages also saw the theoretical side of apologetics taking shape. It largely began with Thomas Aquinas who, in rejecting Anselm's ontological reasoning, established what remains today the primary ways one argues for God's existence—from effect back to its cause. These were hardly brought on by the questions of skeptics.

Religions in the Two Kingdoms (Essays in Honor of the Sixty-Fifth Birthday of Charles L. Manske), ed. Daniel N. Harmelink (Huntington Beach: Tentatio Press, 1999), 299-308.
   [2] See *The Lutheran Study Bible* (CPH, 2009), 1572.

God's existence wasn't really being questioned in that day. But they were still important for thinking about the objective foundation for religious belief.

The real apologetic challenges to the faith in Luther's day were virtually the same as in the Middle Ages. Despite persistent persecution, Jewish populations continued to exist and assert their own anti-Christian polemics and apologetic arguments for Christians to embrace a form of Judaism for gentiles called Sabbatarianism. The challenge of Islam also persisted, only in the sixteenth century, it was a much more pressing matter than it had ever been before, for the Ottoman Turks began pushing deep into the heart of Europe. By 1530, Luther complained that they were at Germany's very doorstep, and he feared that many Christians would, for any number of reasons, be enticed to embrace Islam. To these two great apologetic challenges, Luther wrote a variety of responses.

Interestingly, studies specifically addressing his apologetics all but fail to consider them. Avery Dulles's *History of Apologetics,* for example, argues: "Martin Luther...constructed no formal system of apologetics. Not only would this have been foreign to his main purpose—the inner reform of the Church—but it ran counter to his idea of the relations between faith and reason."[3] At best, continues Dulles, "his system did perhaps make room for a type of apologetic constructed from within faith. The development of such apologetics— which would show the inner power of faith from the standpoint of the believer—would have to wait for authors such as Kierkegaard and Barth, both of whom were strongly influenced by Luther's dynamic and existential concept of reason."[4]

Although he seemed unaware of Dulles's work, this is what Siegbert Becker characterized as an existentialist and neo-orthodox interpretation of Luther in his monograph *The Foolishness of God.* In a chapter entitled "Luther's Apologetics," he summarized the reformer's approach as basically a Biblicist one. "After all is said and done," wrote Becker, "the whole of Luther's apologetics can still adequately be summed up in a sentence which he wrote into the margin of his copy of the works of Peter Lombard, 'Arguments based on reason

---

[3] Avery Dulles, *A History of Apologetics* (Eugene: Wipf and Stock, 1999), 113.
[4] Dulles, 114.

determine nothing, but because Holy Scripture says that it is true, it is true.'"[5]

There is one other primary interpretation, coming from a long-forgotten German Lutheran apologist named Otto Zöckler. His dense volume on the history of apologetics treats Luther briefly, but gets to the heart of the reformer's theology and epistemology in this description: "The best foundation for all defenses of Christianity is expressed in this sentence: Jesus Christ alone satisfies the need for salvation *and* at the same time man's need for truth."[6]

The implications of this have been thoroughly explored and exploited by John Warwick Montgomery. For him, if Luther had an apologetic system, it would start "the search for God...at the connecting link between earth and heaven which exists at the point of the incarnation...absolute truth is available only here.... The *point of departure* must be Christ."[7] Believe what you want, but the method (or system) he has developed, which is probably most completely outlined in his *Tractatus Logico-Theologicus*, derives unapologetically and robustly from evidence to the incarnation to establish an objective epistemological basis for the Christian faith.

Luther's theology does not lead to fideism (faith in faith) and may well permit such a comprehensive apologetic. What is interesting in much, if not all, of the discussions of Luther's view of and approach to apologetics is that none of them actually explore his use of apologetics. Instead, they deduce from his theology what his apologetic might have been had he lived in the modern world or, alternatively, what it would not have been. An example of this is can be found in an article by H. Wayne House in the *Concordia Journal* where he asked (and answered) the question: "How would Luther react to much of modern apologetics?... He would repudiate it....

---

[5] Siegbert W. Becker, *The Foolishness of God: The Place of Reason in the Theology of Martin Luther* (Milwaukee: Northwestern Publishing House, 1982), 191. The chapter from which this quotation comes was originally published (under the same title, "Luther's Apologetics") in the *Concordia Theological Monthly* 29:10 (October 1958): 742-759.

[6] Otto Zöckler, *Geschichte der Apologie des Christentums* (Gütersloh: C. Bertelsmann, 1907), 309-310.

[7] Montgomery, "Lutheranism and the Defense of the Faith," 22.

[He] would say that" an evidential or rational apologetic "caters to a theology of glory."[8]

Such conclusions are speculative. Luther was never faced with the rank unbelief modern apologetics addresses today. One thing that is for certain is that after a thorough reading of Luther, one sees a man who is both principled yet often pragmatic and even creative in his approach to things. There were no atheists in Luther's day— nor were there demythologizing higher critics. But, as has already been mentioned, there were Jews and Muslims. And it is in his work addressing each and on a variety of occasions that we see Luther the reformer of the Christian church operating as apologist for the faith.

Before describing these, though, a brief definition of apologetics and Luther's understanding of the defense of the faith is in order. First, for the purposes of this paper, apologetics is defined as a defense of Christianity over and against objections to it in a context where the objections come from a decidedly non-Christian perspective (and not a different Christian confession). Leander Keyser, a professor of systematic theology and apologetics at Hamma Divinity School in the early twentieth century, helpfully distinguished the former from the latter by describing apologetics as contention with "infidels outside of the Christian Church" and polemics as debate "with heretics within the church."[9] The sainted Kurt Marquart, who was no mean apologist himself, described apologetics as distinct from theology proper. The latter is derived from revelation; apologetics is, in a way, prolegomena to theology. He went on to add that such a prolegomena to theology "is perfectly valid, indeed necessary." Before the non-Christian, it is necessary "to reason from the common ground of public informa- tion and argument."[10] To put it another way, apologetics as generally defined here takes place in a realm where quotations from the New Testament, historical theologians (including Luther or the confes- sions), or ecclesiastical bylaws do not resolve differences. Luther

---

[8] H. Wayne House, "The Value of Reason in Luther's View of Apologetics," *Concordia Journal* 7/2 (1981): 66.

[9] Leander Keyser, *A System of Christian Evidences* (Burlington, IA: The Lutheran Literary Board, 1922), 23.

[10] Kurt Marquart, *Anatomy of an Explosion: A Theological Analysis of the Missouri Synod Conflict* (Fort Wayne: Concordia Theological Seminary Press, 1977), 128.

himself noted in his great commentary on Galatians that when you are in this arena, when you have to "engage in controversy with Jews, Turks, etc.," quoting the Bible is of little use. "You must use all your cleverness and effort and be as profound and subtle a controversialist as possible; for then you are in another area."[11] That is, you must use your reason, you must appeal to facts and be as precise and logical as possible (or at least as the context demands).

Such a task, for Luther, was not merely for specialists, those apologetic wonks who can cite chapter and verse of the Book of Mormon or—maybe worse—the Qur'an, or those who have way too much free time on their hands and can spend countless hours in chat rooms (if there are such things anymore), blogs, or in high-profile debates exposing the irrationality of Richard Dawkins. Nor is it just for seminarians, theologians, or those masquerading as theologians. The apologetic task, for Luther, is for every Christian. Commenting on 1 Peter 3:15, "Sanctify Christ as Lord in your hearts, always being ready to make a defense to everyone who asks you to give a reason for the hope that is in you," Luther wrote. "Here we shall have to admit that St. Peter is addressing these words to all Christians, to priests, lay[people], men and women, young and old, and in whatever station they are. Therefore it follows from this that every Christian should account for his faith and be able to give a reason and an answer when necessary."[12]

Luther's earliest apologetic opponents were the Jews. Not much is known about his personal contact with them, but his early work demonstrates that he was well aware of their historical suffering and persecution and thoroughly acquainted with their beliefs. There is some evidence that he had some personal contact with a few Rabbis and would also have a nasty epistolary exchange with probably the most influential Jew of his day—Josel of Rosheim. The older he got, the more the Jews resisted the gospel, and especially the more Luther learned of Jewish anti-Christian and sensationalist polemics, the more impatient (and agitated) he got. This is the Luther, Luther the anti-semite, that most people know. In his early work, however, he expressed hope that they might be converted. In his lectures on

---

[11] LW 26:29-30.
[12] LW 30:105.

Romans, he wrote that even though they had thrown "Christ out to the Gentiles," he was confident that, should they hear a clear exposition of the gospel from the Old Testament, they might "receive him among the gentiles."[13]

After Luther was thrown out of the Roman Church, rumors started circulating that he had been influenced by Jewish ideas. At the Diet of Nurnberg in 1522, he was even accused of rejecting the virgin birth. His response, *That Christ was Born a Jew* (1523), cleared the air of that and other false accusations. It was also written so that a Jew, too, might find his arguments compelling. He wrote,

> If I had been a Jew and had seen such dolts and blockheads govern and teach the Christian faith, I would sooner have become a hog than a Christian.... They have dealt with the Jews as if they were dogs rather than human beings.... I hope that if one deals in a kindly way with the Jews and instructs them carefully from holy scripture, many of them will become genuine Christians.... When we are inclined to boast of our position we should remember that we are but Gentiles, while the Jews are of the lineage of Christ.[14]

We know of at least one Jew, a man named Bernhard Gipher, who came to study in Wittenberg, who became a Christian after reading Luther's treatise.[15]

Early in the 1530s, despite what he thought were his best efforts, Luther began to grow weary of the general resistance of Jews to the gospel. He had also learned of their efforts to convert Christians in Moravia, Bohemia, and Poland, and he was convinced that the appearance of the Sabbatarians was a result of their activity. So he wrote *Against the Sabbatarians* in 1538 to demonstrate the error of Jewish theology so that Christians would be able to make a defense of the Christian faith. This led to a response from the Jewish community in the form of a booklet that attacked the divinity of Jesus, the virginity of Mary, and Christian exegesis of the Old Testament—to which Luther responded in his notorious works of 1543: *On the Jews*

---

[13] LW 25:430.

[14] LW 45:200-201.

[15] Pekka Huhtinen, "Luther and World Mission: A Review," *Concordia Theological Quarterly* 65/1 (2001): 25n26.

and Their Lies; On the Ineffable Name; and *On the Last Words of Jesus.*
They were Luther's last statement against Jewish theology. And while
the vitriol is inexcusable, it is entirely typical for the context—from
the polemics of both sides. Certainly it is interesting that in less than
three years, right before his death, he would again advocate from the
pulpit that Christians treat the Jews kindly but still insist that the Jews
need to turn from their blasphemy, embrace Christ, and be baptized.
Such was the often paradoxical and conflicted mind of Luther on the
subject of the Jews.

In any case, his apologetic against Judaism was singularly
focused around the person of Jesus and whether he was, in fact,
the promised messiah. From *That Christ Was Born a Jew* to his
later polemics, he advised that since "the Jews do not accept the
evangelists we must confront them with other evidence."[16] He thus
worked primarily from the Old Testament, being careful to show
that he didn't impose a Christological reading upon the text, and
demonstrating that it was necessary for the Messiah to suffer and
die just as, they knew from history, that Jesus suffered and died. He
was convinced that, despite the functional Marcionism of much of
Christianity,[17] the patriarchs and prophets of old were Christians
in faith and fact, though maybe not in name. So he tried to show
and illustrate for Christians who had dealings with Jews "a method
and some passages from Scripture...they should employ in dealing
with them."[18]

For his Jewish audience, he sought to show them prima facie
evidence from their own sacred text of the "true faith" of the
ancient Hebrew people and that Rabbinic theology was based on
tortured grammar and exegesis. You could say he offered a system of Christian evidences for the Jews and potential missionaries
to the Jews. One twentieth-century Luther scholar went so far as
to describe Luther as the "father of Protestant Jewish missions."[19]

---

[16] LW 45:208.
[17] The term is from Daniel L. Guard's "The Church's Scripture and
Functional Marcionism," *Concordia Theological Quarterly* 74 (2010): 209-224.
[18] LW 45:213.
[19] Armas K.E. Holmio, *Martin Luther: Friend or Foe of the Jews* (Chicago:
National Lutheran Council, 1949), 16.

That's a stretch, but there is scholarly consensus that the most fundamental aspect of Luther's writings on the Jews had an "apologetic missionary tendency" to persuade them to return to the faith of their ancient fathers.[20]

But Luther's apologetic contest with Jews wasn't just an argument over the meaning of the Hebrew text. This was, in the estimate of many Hebraists and Old Testament scholars, impressive. Interestingly, Luther also used historical evidence to bolster his argument. In the three works from 1543, he used the gospels not as sacred script but eyewitness testimony alongside ancient Jewish authors such as Josephus and Philo to demonstrate the weakness of Jewish theology and its claims to antiquity and, more positively, to provide evidence from miracle for the messianic credentials of Jesus. "Whoever is not moved by this miraculous spectacle," he wrote, "deserves to remain blind."[21] And in conclusion to his argument against Judaism and apologia for Christianity, he ended by saying: "My essays, I hope, will furnish a Christian (who in any case has no desire to become a Jew) with enough material not only to defend himself against the blind, venomous Jews, but also to become the foe of the Jews" so that they might understand their belief is false.[22]

Luther's apologetic to Judaism was a fairly traditional one, learned from the medieval scholastic tradition that began in the thirteenth century with Raymond Martini, Nicholas of Lyra, Salvagus Prochetus, and the Jewish convert Paul of Burgos. His argument with Islam was likewise part of the scholastic tradition, but included some of his own innovations. It was the expansion of the Ottoman Empire into central Europe that was the catalyst for his engagement with Islam. From 1521 until the end of Luther's life, the Turks forced their way into Hungary with their sights trained on Germany. The 1529 siege of Vienna, in particular, frightened everybody, for as Luther expressed, it placed the Turks and their religion next door to the Holy Roman Empire. Accompanying the annexations of much of Hungary was the Islamization of eastern

---

[20] Mark U. Edwards, *Luther's Last Battles: Politics and Polemics, 1532-1546* (Ithaca: Cornell University Press, 1991), 366.

[21] LW 47:300.

[22] LW 47:305-306.

Europe. The conversion of the cathedral into a mosque in Buda, many thought, was but a foreshadowing of events to come. And Luther was convinced that if the final judgment did not occur soon, the world would go Muslim.

The Ottoman advance and annexation of eastern and parts of central Europe brought Christians and Muslims into close contact. Muslim enclaves were beginning to appear in Hungary. And many Christians who found themselves subject of the Turks were beginning to assume "Islam without having much of a choice in the matter."[23] There were even reports of violent efforts to proselytize among the inhabitants of southern Hungary. Some willingly embraced Islam. I have "heard and read," wrote Luther, "that many Christians have committed apostasy and willingly and without force believed the faith of the Turks or Muhammad."[24]

The expansion of what Luther called the Muhammadan Empire made it vital for Christians to be able to respond intelligently to Islam. So he began to write on it. His first work was entitled *On War against the Turk*. This little book was published on the eve of the siege of Vienna. Its chief purpose was to explain and encourage war—properly conceived according to the doctrine of just war—against the Turks. It likewise provided a little synopsis of Islamic teaching. Shortly afterwards, he penned another little work entitled *A Muster Sermon against the Turk*, the second half of which was written for, as Luther wrote, "Germans already captive in Turkey or those who might still become captive."[25] He provided basic advice to Christians on how to live as Christians amidst Muslims, especially under the restrictions of sharia law. Over a decade later, after he helped get a Latin translation of the Qur'an and other Islamic literature published so that Christians could learn about Islam from primary texts, he got to work on a very loose translation of what was the most influential medieval scholastic

---

[23] Allen Hertz, "Muslims, Christians and Jews in Sixteenth-Century Belgrade," *The Mutual Effects of the Islamic and Judeo-Christian Worlds: The East European Pattern,* eds. Abraham Ascher, Tibor Halasi-Kun, and Béla Király (New York: Brooklyn College Press, 1979), 149.

[24] WA 30/2:185.

[25] WA 30/2:185.

apologetic directed against Islam. He entitled the resulting work *A Refutation of the Qur'an* and published it for two reasons. First, he explained, so that "whether the book arrives through print or its arguments through the mouths of Christians struggling against the Turks, that those Christians who are now or in the future under the Turks might protect themselves against Islam, even if they are not able to protect themselves against his sword."[26] He hoped it would equip Christians in the task of apologetics—so that, he wrote, they might be "lion hearts" in defense of the gospel.[27] Secondly, though he did not have much confidence in this, he hoped its arguments might be used to bring those "led astray by the Qur'an and Islam back to God."[28]

The *Refutation* followed a distinct method for arguing with Islam. As Luther put it: "[O]ne must not deal with Muslims at first by asserting and defending the high articles of our faith, but rather with this approach: take and diligently work with their Qur'an, demonstrating their theology to be false and useless."[29] Afterward, one should argue for the veracity of Christianity. More than the first half of the *Refutation* argues against the Qur'an by showing that it cannot be construed as a legitimate revelation from God by a rational person for the following reasons: The Qur'an claims, in a way, to supersede the Torah, Psalms, and Gospel. But "neither the Old or New Testament bear witness to it or Muhammad, it does not cohere with any biblical doctrine, it contradicts itself, it has not been confirmed by miraculous signs, it even contradicts common sense reason, there are obvious lies in it, it promotes murder, it is disorderly, it is shameful, and the history of its composition is dubious."[30]

The last few chapters of the *Refutation* are the most interesting, for Luther attempted to demonstrate Christian doctrine from a few ambiguous passages of the Qur'an. He suggested such a thing could be done for he believed the Holy Spirit caused Muhammad to

---

[26] WA 53:392.
[27] *Luthers Werke: Briefwechsel* (Weimar: H. Böhlau, 1930–1985), 10:162.
[28] WA 53:278.
[29] WA 53:284.
[30] WA 53:378.

unwittingly express Christian doctrine. For example, he pointed out the consistent use of the first person plural with reference to God's speech. From this, he used passages like Qur'an 4:171, where Jesus is referred to as the word of God (*kalimatullah*) born of a virgin through the work of the spirit of God (*ruhallah*) to suggest the Qur'an can be made to express a convoluted doctrine of the trinity. The Qur'an also suggests that the Torah, Psalms, and Gospel are legitimate revelations from God. Muslims invented the doctrine of *tahrif* to explain the obvious contradictions, effectively contradicting the Qur'an's claims. He then added to this that the biblical books should have priority and, at the very least, Muslims were compelled by their own Scripture to read and believe them.

The *Refutation* is certainly an interesting text. And for the time it was the most sophisticated apologetic against Islam available. The Latin text from which Luther translated and adopted would persist and inform the first modern apologetic treatise about a century later written by Hugo Grotius entitled *On the Truth of the Christian Religion*. The real value of it for understanding Luther's approach to apologetics, though, is that it suggests a much more pragmatic Luther than do those who would characterize him as a Biblicist. And that he borrowed and took his cues from a scholastic treatise suggests he was no pre-Kierkegaardian existentialist. Rather, he was a traditional apologist, who received and passed on the basic scholastic approach to apologetics against Jews and Muslims, mixed with a few of his own innovations.

It is undeniable that Luther used and recognized the need for apologetics. He, in fact, believed all Christians should be prepared to give a reason for the hope within them. It would be strange for a man so confident in the objectivity of the faith to dismiss it. This—and not the existentialism or neo-orthodox influences that came later—was the spirit of the reformers. They weren't dogmatists (though they held fast to certain dogmas). They kept an open mind, relative to the time. Luther, for example, always kept himself in check by asking the question, "Am I alone wise?" Lyndal Roper describes him this way: "For Luther, doubt always accompanied faith.... [I]n one debate, Luther suddenly became unsure that he was right, and he left the room, falling on his bed and praying.... He was utterly engaged in the subject under discussion, and shaken to the core by the thought that he might have been mistaken." This was characteristic, she contends, of his "extraordinary openness" and "honest willingness to put everything on the line."[31]

Luther and the other reformers were convinced the truth was discoverable, even by the unregenerate. The second Martin wrote,

> It is absolutely clear that the mind in itself has not been deprived of all understanding, and there remains in even unregenerate men some ability of the mind to perceive and judge those things which are subject to reason and the senses.... God willed that some of these gifts should remain in the mind, whence man could consider both what God is and what he is like; likewise, in order that there can be instruction to lead us to Christ.[32]

Or, as Luther put it in the catechism, "God has given us our reason and our senses and still preserves them." The thesis that scholars like Avery Dulles have advanced, that the reformer was skeptical of apologetics, is simply untenable. So, too, is Becker's thesis that Luther would only go as far as biblical proof texting, even if it is done in such a way as to show the internal consistency of Christian doctrine.

It should also be added that, in addition to his focused use of apologetics against the unbelievers of his day, Luther's theology was not so closed that he would reject wholesale the way apologetics developed in the centuries after him. He was very much a part of the scholastic apologetic tradition, and so he could not conceive of an epistemology being developed apart from certain theistic ontological assumptions, as so many of the thinkers of the Enlightenment tried to do. (They failed, by the way. There is no such thing as absolute neutrality, especially in the realm of religion.)

Nevertheless, despite his premodern worldview, there is enough material in Luther to suggest he was confident that inductive reasoning from the effects and teleology of the cosmos would lead one to conclude that a deity caused it all. For example, he wrote:

---

[31] Lyndal Roper, *Martin Luther: Renegade and Prophet* (New York: Random House, 2017), 410.

[32] Martin Chemnitz, *Loci Theologici*, trans. J.A.O. Preus (St. Louis: Concordia Publishing House, 1989), 233.

The more observant among the philosophers drew from this source [the cosmos] what is in truth not an insignificant proof: that all things are done and guided, not planlessly but by divine providence, inasmuch as the movements of the masses on high and of the heaven are so definite and unique. Who would say that they are accidental or purely a matter of nature, when the objects fashioned by artisans—such as round or three-cornered or six-cornered columns—are not accidental but the result of a definite plan and skill.[33]

There are plenty of other places in Luther where other forms of the *a posteriori* arguments for God's existence are expressed. To be sure, at best these arguments only established the existence of a "Supreme Being." "It is [still] interesting to observe," however, wrote N. Arne Bendtz, "how far Luther sometimes can go in recognizing man's knowledge of God unaided by revelation. It is raised above all doubts that man's knowledge leads him to the acceptance of the existence of God."[34]

In Luther's mind, natural knowledge of God served two purposes. On the one hand, it kept "man from becoming like brutes which perish. It constantly reminds him of a higher standard than is attainable under the mere light of Nature...and it impels man ever onward in his search for truth and for God." On the other hand, natural knowledge or natural theology "is like writing that needs the intervention of a lens in order to be legible by one whose sight is failing. Some facts indeed are known, but they are misapprehended and viewed in wrong relations; and the most important are entirely wanting."[35]

For Luther, then, and as we all ought to know, lucid and certain knowledge of God comes from his word, particularly in the person of his word made flesh who dwelt among us. "This is why Paul makes such a frequent practice of linking Jesus Christ with God the Father," he wrote, "to teach us what is the true...religion. It does not begin

---

[33] LW 1:25.

[34] N. Arne Bendtze, "Faith and Knowledge in Luther's Theology," in *Reformation Studies: Sixteen Essays in Honor of Roland H. Bainton,* ed. Franklin H. Littell (Richmond, VA: John Knox Press, 1962), 22-23.

[35] Henry Eyster Jacobs, *A Summary of the Christian Faith* (Philadelphia: General Council Publication House, 1905), 7-8.

at the top, as all other religions do; it begins at the bottom. It bids us climb up by Jacob's ladder.... Therefore...put away all speculation about the Majesty, all thoughts of works, traditions, and philosophy.... And you must run directly to the manger and the mother's womb, embrace this infant and virgin's child in your arms, and look at him, born, being nursed, growing up, going about in human society, teaching, dying, rising again, ascending above all the heavens, and having authority over all things."[36]

So, it seems that if Luther had developed an apologetic system to demonstrate that Christianity was not a cleverly devised myth, he would have approached it from the incarnation, factually or historically, for this is what sets Christianity apart from all other religions and worldviews. And this wasn't just a dogmatic or doctrinal point he was making. He believed it was also the tremendous epistemological difference that Christianity makes. Apologetics, then, was or ought to be, for Luther, an essential part of the life of the mind. It was especially essential for those in ecclesiastical vocations or public ministry. In his preface to the Qur'an, he wrote,

> There can be no thought of leisure, especially for those of us who teach in the church. We must fight everywhere against the armies of the devil. How many different enemies have we seen in our own time?— the defenders of the pope's idols, the Jews, a multitude of Anabaptist monstrosities, the party of Servetus/Unitarians, and others [we might add atheists, agnostics, maybe democrats and with Luther we could say] Let us now prepare ourselves against Muhammad as well. But what will we be able to say concerning things of which we are ignorant? That is why it is beneficial for learned people to read the writings of their enemies—so that they may more accurately refute, strike, and overturn those writings, so that they may be able to correct some of them or at least to fortify our own people with stronger arguments.[37]

Apologists can certainly be quirky, obsessive, and even myopic at times. That's no reason to scuttle the enterprise, and it's no reason for the Lutheran to puff up his or her chest and act as if they had Luther's approval (as if Luther's approval is needed, anyway). For

---

[36] LW 26:30.
[37] WA 53:572.

Luther and his heirs really do have a word for the world, even the world of unbelief. It's especially to the latter, like Luther to the Jews and the distant Turk, that the apologist especially speaks. How does he speak? In a creative and factually persuasive way, so that, as St. Paul put it to King Agrippa, he might persuade those who heard or read him to be Christians.

Can a Historian Explain the Empty Tomb with the Resurrection of Jesus?

No historian doubts Julius Caesar was assassinated on the Ides of March in 44 BC, and rarely do they question Jesus of Nazareth's crucifixion a little less than a century later. It is, as one skeptic put it, the one thing about Jesus that is "as sure as anything historical can be."[1] When it comes to Jesus' resurrection, though, there is little consensus. Few doubt he was buried and that the tomb was empty three days later. But, for many, the general presumption is that historical approaches to the life of Jesus cannot explain the empty tomb by appealing to the resurrection.

Why? The evidence is the same for it as the crucifixion. (It is even stronger than the evidence for Julius Caesar's assassination.) Yet, while the death of Jesus on a cross is believable, the resurrection is not. This chapter explores the reasons a historian might make such a claim by exposing the philosophical assumptions behind what is often called the "historical problem of miracles." It then describes the assumptions of historical research and the implications they have on the empty tomb. The result will be a basic yet essential introduction to historical thinking and the resurrection.[2]

---

[1] John Dominic Crossan, *Jesus: A Revolutionary Biography* (New York: Harper Collins, 1991), 145.

[2] For a book-length treatment, see Michael Licona, *The Resurrection of Jesus: A New Historiographical Approach* (Downers Grove: IVP Academic, 2010).

HUME, HISTORICAL RESEARCH, AND MIRACLES

The origin of the discussion about historical research and what it is capable of describing relative to the case of miracles can be traced back to the eighteenth-century Scottish philosopher and historian named David Hume (1711-1776) and his celebrated work entitled *An Enquiry Concerning Human Understanding*. Hume wrote the book to advance a robust empiricist epistemology and applied it to a variety of fields of research, including history and religion. He was no friend of the latter. "[O]ne of his most basic philosophical objectives," writes Paul Russell, was "to unmask and discredit the doctrines and dogmas of orthodox religious belief."[3] So, recognizing that the veracity of Christianity rested on the resurrection of Jesus, Hume went after it by attacking the legitimacy of claims that miracles of whatever sort have occurred and can be demonstrated by the historical method.

There are two parts to his argument. First, he reasoned philosophically: "A miracle is a violation of the laws of nature; and as a firm and unalterable experience has established these laws, the proof against a miracle, from the very nature of the fact, is as entire as any argument from experience can possibly be imagined."[4] That is, the normal, everyday experience of human beings suggests that miracles are not part of the natural or normal order of things. The order that humans observe in nature is, he presumed, static and determined by natural, physical laws. These laws are fixed. They do not change; nor can they be suspended. Therefore, the very concept of a miracle—defined by Hume as a "violation" of these laws—makes their occurrence unbelievable, if not virtually impossible and entirely unbelievable.

Hume then applied his philosophy to claims that a miraculous event had actually occurred. He wrote, "The plain consequence is (and it is a general maxim worthy of our attention) that no testimony is sufficient to establish a miracle unless the testimony be

---

[3] Paul Russell, "Hume on Religion," *The Stanford Encyclopedia of Philosophy* (Winter 2014 Edition), Edward N. Zalta (ed.), URL = <http://plato.stanford.edu/archives/win2014/entries/hume-religion/>.

[4] David Hume, *An Inquiry Concerning Human Understanding* (New York: The Liberal Arts Press, 1955), 122.

of such a kind that its falsehood would be more miraculous than the fact which it endeavors to establish."[5] Because of the high (and almost certain) unlikelihood of a miracle ever occurring, no testimony—directly from eyewitnesses or reports based on eyewitness testimony—can be sufficient enough to merit belief unless the reports become more incredible if the events they purport to describe were untrue. Or, in other words, the less incredible (or miraculous) explanation of an event is always to be preferred even if it contradicts good eyewitness testimony.

It was, in his mind, always more likely that eyewitnesses reporting miracles had lied or been mistaken. So, in the case of a claim that a resurrection occurred, he suggested:

> I immediately consider with myself whether it be more probable that this person would either deceive or be deceived, or that the fact which he relates should really have happened. I weigh the one miracle against the other, and according to the superiority which I discover I pronounce my decision, and always reject the greater miracle. If the falsehood of his testimony would be more miraculous than the event which he relates, then, and not till then, can he pretend to command my belief or opinion.[6]

Hume's argument provoked a variety of responses from philosophers and Christian apologists alike almost immediately after its publication.[7] One of the most well known was the satirical *Historic Doubts Relative to Napoleon Buonaparte*, where Richard Whately (1787-1863) took Hume's principles, applied them to the extraordinary life of the then-exiled emperor of the French, and found that the same line of reasoning forced one to doubt his existence.[8] The irony was that Napoleon was still living at the time. The same approach was also applied to the extraordinary life of Abraham Lincoln and incredible events at the Battle of Bunker

---

[5] Hume, 123.

[6] Hume, 123-24.

[7] See James Fieser, ed., *Early Responses to Hume's Writings on Religion*, 2 vols. (New York: Bloomsbury Publishing, 2005).

[8] See Craig Parton, *Richard Whately: A Man for All Seasons* (Edmonton: Canadian Institute for Law, Theology, and Public Policy), 1997.

Hill.[9] They all served to illustrate the philosophical and methodological weakness of Hume's maxim that no testimony—contemporary or historical—was sufficient enough to warrant acceptance
of an incredible or miraculous event like a resurrection as a historical fact.

Despite the wide array of historical and contemporary criticism
in works like C.S. Lewis' *Miracles* (1947/1960) and John Earman's
Hume's Abject Failure (2000), the eighteenth-century skeptic's
influence persists—even in the realm of theology. John Warwick
Montgomery notes, "Hume's *Enquiry* can be said without exagger-
ation to mark the end of the era of classical Christian apologetics."[10]
Jesus' miracles were a mainstay in the apologetic tradition until
the eighteenth century, where especially the resurrection was mar-
shaled as undeniable evidence for the deity of Jesus and therefore
the compelling nature of his teachings. But after Hume, that ceased
to be the case. His influence is still pervasive and remains especially
strong in biblical scholarship, "endorsed, explicitly or implicitly, in
many contemporary studies of the historical Jesus...and the New
Testament."[11] A contemporary version of it is on display in what has
been described as the standard text for introductory New Testament
courses—Bart Ehrman's *New Testament: A Historical Introduction
to the Early Christian Writings.*

EHRMAN, HISTORICAL RESEARCH, AND MIRACLES

Ehrman's *Introduction* treats the New Testament as the best
available source for understanding the life of Jesus and the early
Christian church worthy of the historian's attention. The miracles its authors describe, however, are not. The reasons are set

---

[9] See Oliver Price Buel, *The Abraham Lincoln Myth* (New York: The Mascot
Publishing Co, 1894) and Charles Hudson, *Doubts Concerning the Battle of
Bunker Hill* (Boston, James Munroe and Co., 1857).

[10] John Warwick Montgomery, "Science, Theology, and the Miraculous," in
Faith Founded on Fact: Essays in Evidential Apologetics (Edmonton: Canadian
Institute for Law, Theology, and Public Policy, 2001), 44.

[11] Timothy McGrew, "Miracles", *The Stanford Encyclopedia of Philosophy*
(Winter 2015 Edition), Edward N. Zalta (ed.), URL = <http://plato.stanford.edu
/archives/win2015/entries/miracles/>.

forth in the excursus entitled "The Historian and the Problem of Miracle".[12]

Ehrman begins his case against historians being able to acknowledge miracles with the assertion: "Even if miracles *are* possible, there is no way for the historian who sticks strictly to the canons of historical evident [*sic*] to *show* that they have ever happened." The argument he advances to support this is what he calls "the 'historical' problem of miracle." This is an attempt to distinguish it from the fairly obvious presumptuousness of "the 'philosophical' problem of miracles." The latter assumes miracles do not occur, even that the very term is nonsensical, and thus rules out the miracles that Jesus performed.

This is very much the basis of Hume's first argument, namely miracles are a violation of the laws of nature. The laws of nature are, from the uniform experience of humans, firm and unalterable. Nothing—not even eyewitness testimony, regardless of how good— would rise to the level (nowhere near it) of considering the claims that a miracle occurred.

Ehrman's argument is only slightly different. He begins by defining a miracle not as a violation of the laws of nature but an event "that contradict[s] the normal workings of nature in such a way as to be virtually beyond belief and to require an acknowledgment that supernatural forces have been at work." Immediately, he claims, this poses a "major stumbling block" for historians. They "have no access to supernatural forces but only to the public record, that is, to events that can be observed and interpreted by any reasonable person of any religious persuasion." And this precludes a supernatural explanation for extraordinary events.

Why? "If accepting the occurrence of a miracle requires belief in the supernatural realm, and historians by the very nature of their craft can speak only about events of the natural world (which are accessible to observers of every kind) how can they ever certify that an event *outside* the natural order—that is, a miracle—occurred?"

---

[12] Bart Ehrman, *The New Testament: A Historical Introduction to the Early Christian Writings,* fourth ed. (New York: Oxford University Press, 2008), 240-45. All subsequent quotations in this section, unless otherwise noted, come from this excursus.

Ehrman is cautious here not to appear presumptuous by ruling out the possibility of a miracle. He acknowledges, "I'm willing to grant that miracles…can and do happen." He just does not believe there can ever be sufficient evidence to establish that one has occurred, and he explains by comparing the historical discipline to the empirical sciences.

On the basis of and over the course of their experiments and empirical observations, scientists offer predictions of what will happen in the future. Historians work by describing singular, unrepeatable events of the past. Historical descriptions of what happened in the past are, by the unrepeatable and particular nature of their work, much less reliable than scientific descriptions of what will happen in the future. "Since historians cannot repeat the past in order to establish what has probably happened," he concludes, "there will always be less certainty in their conclusions.… And the farther back you go in history, the harder it is to mount a convincing case."

This is especially the case with a miracle. Irrespective of when it allegedly happened, the evidence will always be so problematic and weak by comparison to what normally happens as to preclude the historian from affirming that such an event occurred. Miracles are unrepeatable events that defy what normally occurs in the natural world. They are thus extremely improbable. Yet, the historian works in the realm of what is probable, argues Ehrman. Thus,

> [M]iracles create an inescapable dilemma for historians. Since historians can only establish what probably happened in the past, and the chances of a miracle happening, by definition, are infinitesimally remote, historians can never demonstrate that a miracle probably happened.… Even if there are otherwise good sources for a miraculous event, the very nature of the historical discipline prevents the historian from arguing for its probability.

What this all means, then, is that the best explanation for the empty tomb on Easter morning is most probably not that Jesus rose from the dead.

The historian—if he is abiding by the canons of historical research and not imposing his or her faith on the evidence—has to remain neutral on the question of miracles, especially the resurrection.

During a debate with apologist William Lane Craig in 2006, Ehrman put it this way:

> I'm not saying it didn't happen; but if it did happen, it would be a miracle. The resurrection claims are claims that not only that Jesus' body came back alive; it came back alive never to die again. That's a violation of what naturally happens, every day, time after time, millions of times a year. What are the chances of that happening? Well, it'd be a miracle. In other words, it'd be so highly improbable that we can't account for it by natural means. A theologian may claim that it's true, and to argue with the theologian we'd have to argue on theological grounds because there are no historical grounds to argue on. Historians can only establish what probably happened in the past, and by definition a miracle is the least probable occurrence. And so, by the very nature of the canons of historical research, we can't claim historically that a miracle probably happened. By definition, it probably didn't. And history can only establish what probably did.[13]

There are, he contends, a number of other much more plausible explanations (because they are not supernatural) that have just as much going for them as the accounts found in the New Testament. For an example he makes up the following story to explain the empty tomb.

> Jesus gets buried by Joseph of Arimathea. Two of Jesus' family members are upset that an unknown Jewish leader has buried the body. In the dead of night, these two family members raid the tomb, taking the body off to bury it for themselves. But Roman soldiers on the lookout see them carrying the shrouded corpse through the streets, they confront them, and they kill them on the spot. They throw all three bodies into a common burial plot, where within three days these bodies are decomposed beyond recognition. The tomb then is empty. People go to the tomb, they find it empty, they come to think that Jesus was raised from the dead, and they start thinking they've seen him because they know he's been raised because his tomb is empty.[14]

---

[13] http://www.reasonablefaith.org/is-there-historical-evidence-for-the
-resurrection-of-jesus-the-craig-ehrman#ixzz40OiMyHUd

[14] http://www.reasonablefaith.org/is-there-historical-evidence-for-the
-resurrection-of-jesus-the-craig-ehrman#ixzz40Ok6EIDu

Ehrman does not believe this story is true, but he does claim that it is much more reasonable and therefore believable than the biblical one.

EHRMAN'S PHILOSOPHICAL PROBLEM

There are a variety of problems associated with Ehrman's rejection of miracles as verifiable by the historian. They begin already with his definition of a miracle as an event "that contradict[s] the normal workings of nature in such a way as to be virtually beyond belief and to require an acknowledgment that supernatural forces have been at work." Why would such an event be, by definition, beyond belief? Ehrman notes in his excursus that there are many Christian historians who do believe miracles have occurred. "When they think or do this," he asserts, "they do so not in their capacity as historians but in their capacity as believers."[15] That is, their prior belief in miracles—and not the evidence—leads them to believe miracles such as the resurrection occurred.

This may be true of *some* Christian historians. But assuming for the moment that there is good historical evidence for a miracle such as the resurrection, is it not just as legitimate to assert that historians who deny the resurrection do so because it does not fit their assumptions about what normally occurs in nature and they are therefore guilty of the same circular reasoning? While Ehrman does not overtly argue that proper historical research requires a commitment to a naturalist worldview, he does require it to follow a naturalist methodology, and in doing is the implicit assumption of naturalism. The only reason an event that contradicts the normal workings of nature would be beyond belief is only if one is not permitted to acknowledge that a supernatural force explains the event because of some prior commitment to naturalism.[16]

Ehrman is right though in maintaining that what happened in the past can only be known to the historian by the evidence. Even here,

---

[15] Ehrman, 244.

[16] For a rigorous exposure of the philosophical naturalism behind methodological naturalism, see Alvin Plantina's two-part essay "Methodological Naturalism?" in the online journal *Origins and Design* 18:1 & 2 (1997) at http://www.arn.org/odesign/odesign.htm.

however, his naturalist assumptions get in the way. This can be seen in his repeated use of terms that imply the probability of something. Miracles are "infinitesimally remote," he assumes, because they defy the way nature normally works. Therefore, even "otherwise good" or sound historical sources that contain regular, believable events are unreliable at the point they describe miraculous events. Because miracles are "infinitesimally remote," they are highly improbable. Historians work in the realm of probability when it comes to explaining the past. This, in Ehrman's presentation of the historical problem of miracles, prevents the historian from considering the evidence that a miracle happened or at least places it in a realm of inquiry that is beyond the reach of the historian. In the end, Ehrman sums his view of the possibility of miracles as events that, "[e]ven if they have happened, they are (in common parlance) *impossible*."[17] This is telling. It makes plain that his real problem with miracles is, in the final analysis, a philosophical one masquerading as a historical one. A case could even be made that he has elevated his philosophical assumptions to the level of an ideology such that facts which, under normal historical procedure, require a miraculous (or even anomalous) explanation, are in a circular way interpreted by the initial assumptions. This is not the way historians approach evidence. It is, however, the way ideologues, propagandists, and conspiracy theorists do.

HISTORICAL RESEARCH AND THE EMPTY TOMB

So what do the "canons" of historical research tell us about miracles? When it comes to the basic assumptions historians make about the nature of historical research, the answer is nothing. Like other fields of knowledge, the historian assumes that a world exists outside of our minds, and that it exists independent of our beliefs about it. Yet, particulars about it can be discovered and known by a careful and unbiased investigation of it.[18] What the historian tries to avoid is

---

[17] Ehrman, 240.

[18] For a great defense of the historical method yielding justifiable knowledge and truth, see Richard J. Evans, *In Defense of History* (New York: W.W. Norton, 1999), and for an overview of how historians have approached their discipline from ancient to modern times, see Jeremy D. Popkin, *From Herodotus to H-Net: The Story of Historiography* (New York: Oxford University Press, 2016).

assuming what sort of interpretation of the evidence before exam-
ining it is most likely the case. The historian explains the past by
determining what the most likely explanation is of a particular event,
in view of or from the evidence. The gold standard for assessing the
veracity of a historian's description of the past, then, is not coherence with his or her other beliefs about the world. Rather, it is how
well it corresponds to the evidence that is specific to the event under
investigation.[19]

What, then, can the historian say concerning the end of Jesus'
life? That he died by crucifixion is almost universally acknowledged.[20]
With the exception of what amount to conspiracy theories, so too is
his burial in a tomb that was discovered empty three days later.[21] The
question we are left with is *why* the tomb was empty. The way a

---

[19] See C. Behan McCullagh, *Justifying Historical Descriptions* (New York:
Cambridge University Press, 1984).

[20] Historically, the Islamic tradition has, with few exceptions, denied the
crucifixion of Jesus. This is not for historical reasons, though, but because the
Qur'an implies as much. See Todd Lawson, *The Crucifixion and the Qur'an:
A Study in the History of Muslim Thought* (Oxford: OneWorld Publications,
2009).

[21] This is not just what the Gospels and other New Testament documents
say. The earliest attempts to discredit Christianity assume it to be the case as
well. In the second and third centuries, Justin Martyr (*Dialogue with Trypho
the Jew*, 108) and Tertullian (*De Spectaculis*, 30) explain that the Jews were still
circulating the story of the disciples stealing the body of Jesus, just as they did
in the days following the discovery of the empty tomb (see Matthew 28:11-15).
Later Jewish polemics (fifth century, at the earliest) likewise acknowledge Jesus'
body "was not found in the grave where he had been buried," but rather than
the disciples stealing the body, they alleged that a gardener removed it and
buried it in the sand (see Morris Goldstein, *Jesus in the Jewish Tradition* [New
York: MacMillan, 1950], 148-54). There is no evidence that suggests Jesus' body
remained in the tomb. Had it been there, the Jewish or Roman officials would
have exhumed and publicly displayed it to shut the mouths of the Christians
who based their faith and their preaching on the resurrection. There have, of
course, been some desperate attempts to explain away and deny the empty
tomb by modern academics. But their wild conjecture and invalid historical
inferences cannot compete with the evidence, all of which acknowledges that
the tomb was empty (see, for example, Peter Kirby, "The Case Against the
Empty Tomb," in *The Empty Tomb: Jesus Beyond the Grave,* ed. Robert Price
and Jeffrey Jaw Lowder [Amherst: Prometheus Press, 2005], 233-60). For all the

historian proceeds to answer it is by assessing the evidence and offering the most probable explanation as determined by the evidence and not *a priori* speculation about what is possible.

What evidence do we have that would explain the empty tomb? There are a surprising amount of relevant literary sources from biblical to non-Christian texts that need to be considered.[22] But the best evidence comes from the canonical gospels. They are all—in their own unique ways—credible biographies of Jesus written by eyewitnesses or the companions of eyewitnesses.[23]

The authors provide the historian a tremendous amount of detail concerning Jesus' life including accounts of Jesus appearing to his disciples three days after his death. They even include material that should have been omitted, especially if they were trying to persuade a first-century audience of something that did not happen.

For example, all four gospels describe women as the first to visit the empty tomb and see the resurrected Jesus (Matthew 28:1-10; Mark 16:1-8 [9-11]; Luke 24:1-12; John 20:1-18). This is interesting since, in their context, a woman's testimony was regarded as irrelevant and unreliable.[24] And yet, they still included it. Why? The most likely—indeed it is hard to conceive of any other—explanation is that it is what happened.[25]

The gospel writers "could not afford to risk inaccuracies (not to speak of willful manipulation of the facts), which would at once be exposed by those who would be only too glad to do so."[26] The hostility Christianity faced almost immediately all but guarantees that they

───────────────

evidence supporting the empty tomb, see William Lane Craig, "The Historicity of the Empty Tomb of Jesus," *New Testament Studies* 31 (1985): 39-67.

[22] See Licona, *The Resurrection*, 199-276.

[23] See Richard Bauckham, *Jesus and the Eyewitnesses: The Gospels as Eyewitness Testimony* (Grand Rapids: Eerdmans, 2008) and, among others, Mark D. Roberts, *Can We Trust the Gospels? Investigating the Reliability of Matthew, Mark, Luke, and John* (Wheaton: Crossway Books, 2007).

[24] See, for example, Josephus, *Antiquities*, 4.8.15.

[25] See Richard Bauckham, "The Women at the Tomb: The Credibility of Their Story," http://richardbauckham.co.uk/uploads/Accessible/The%20 Women%20&%20the%20Resurrection.pdf

[26] F.F. Bruce, *The New Testament Documents: Are They Reliable?* (Grand Rapids: Eerdmans, 1960), 45.

did not invent the story of Jesus rising from the dead. For both the Roman and Jewish officials in first-century Jerusalem had the means, motive, and every opportunity to debunk it.

They did try. Matthew 28:11-15 records that after the events of Easter morning—the stone being inexplicably rolled away and the tomb being empty—the guards that had been placed to keep it secure,

> went into the city and told the chief priests all that had taken place. And when they had assembled with the elders and taken counsel, they gave a sufficient sum of money to the soldiers and said, "Tell people, 'His disciples came by night and stole him away while we were asleep.' And if this comes to the governor's ears, we will satisfy him and keep you out of trouble." So they took the money and did as they were directed. And this story has been spread among the Jews to this day.[27]

This is the only other account of the empty tomb for which we have historical evidence. But Matthew tells us the story was contrived. While he might be considered partisan, it is still hard to imagine the disciples' doing what the Jews alleged. They would have had to do it when a security detail consisting of at least four guards was stationed in front of the tomb.[28] Additionally, had they stolen the body, there is no explanation for why they spent the rest of their lives promoting what they knew to be a lie and then, in the case of many of them, being tortured and executed for it without a single one of them exposing what would probably be the world's greatest conspiracy.

It would also be difficult for a historian to explain the growth or even the existence of the church if Jesus merely died and remained dead. It was, after all, the resurrection that convinced the disciples to

---

[27] All biblical quotations come from *The Holy Bible, English Standard Version* (Wheaton: Crossway, 2001). Justin Martyr (*Dialogue with Trypho the Jew,* 108) and Tertullian (*De Spectaculis,* 30) explain that the Jews were still circulating the story of the disciples stealing the body of Jesus.

[28] It is unclear from Matthew 27:65 whether the guards were Roman or a Temple security detail. If the former, it would have consisted of at least four (see William Smith, *Dictionary of Greek and Roman Antiquities* [Boston: Little, Brown, and Company, 1859)], 250). If the latter, it would have been ten (see Alfred Edersheim, *The Temple: Its Ministry and Services as They Were At the Time of Jesus* [London: The Religious Tract, 1874], 119).

believe Jesus' teachings and emboldened them to preach the gospel of Christianity, with the resurrection itself constituting its earliest and most central proclamation regarding the crucified Christ Jesus.[29]

They also treated the resurrection as *the* event upon which Christianity stands or falls. In 1 Corinthians 15:14-17, for example, Paul wrote,

> And if Christ has not been raised, then our preaching is in vain and your faith is in vain. We are even found to be misrepresenting God, because we testified about God that he raised Christ, whom he did not raise if it is true that the dead are not raised. For if the dead are not raised, not even Christ has been raised. And if Christ has not been raised, your faith is futile and you are still in your sins.

Given the crucifixion and resurrection were the heart and soul of the Christian message from the very beginning and the church began its preaching in and around Jerusalem (Luke 24:33-35; Acts 2:24-25, 31-32; 3:15; 4:1-2, 10, 33), it is extraordinary that the numerous enemies of Christianity did not simply produce the body of Jesus to shut it down. Again, they had ample opportunity and the ability to do so, especially since on several occasions the apostles were in their custody.

The Romans, who regarded Christianity as a pernicious superstition, and the Jews, who began killing Christians well before the Romans did (as in the stoning of Stephen, see Acts 7:54-60), could not discredit the message of Christianity even though it would have been easily discredited. This, however, has not stopped antagonists of Christianity from attempting to discredit on factual, historical grounds today. A wide variety of alternative explanations for the empty tomb apart from the resurrection have been proposed. Since the late eighteenth century, a number of "swoon theories" have posited that Jesus did not die on the cross.[30] Instead, he passed out and, appearing dead, was buried. Then, somehow, beset with multiple, complex, mortal wounds, he was revived and made his way out of

---

[29] See 1 Clement 42:3.

[30] Perhaps the most famous book advocating the swoon hypothesis is Hugh Schonfield's *The Passover Plot: A New Interpretation of the Life and Death of Jesus* (New York: Bernard Geis Associates, 1964).

a sealed tomb, eluding an armed sentry. Others have suggested that the witnesses of the empty tomb went to the wrong tomb or that Jesus' body was placed in the wrong tomb, and when his disciples visited the right grave, which was empty, they assumed he rose from the dead.[31] And another one claims that the eyewitnesses really did believe they saw Jesus alive after his death, but in reality they were all hallucinating.[32] The foremost problem with all of them is that none of them correspond to the evidence in the historical record. They all basically amount to conspiracy theories.

CONCLUSION

The evidence from history is quite clear about certain facts pertaining to Jesus. He was crucified and died on a Roman cross.[33] He did not swoon. The guarded tomb in which he was placed was empty three days later. The only historical rejection of the reports that he rose from the dead by suggesting that the disciples stole the body was merely an assertion contrived by the enemies of Jesus. The disciples did not have the means, motive, or the opportunity to steal the body. Concerning the eyewitness reports of the resurrection, the extant ones have been well preserved in the four canonical gospels. All but one (John) of the twelve apostles (including Paul but precluding Judas) and eyewitnesses of the resurrected Jesus (e.g., Matthias and Mark), according to historical sources and tradition, went to their death standing firm on the claim that what they bore witness to was factual. Had they invented the story, one of them would have caved during their various trials and subsequent executions.

Any historical inquiry into the issue of Jesus' resurrection has all this (and even more) positive evidence to consider. There is no real substantial evidence to the contrary. The historical discipline requires that explanations of what happened in the past follow the trail of

[31] See, for example, P. Gardner-Smith, *The Narratives of the Resurrection* (London: Methuen Press, 1926), 134-39.

[32] See, for example, Gerd Lüdemann, *The Resurrection of Jesus* (Minneapolis: Fortress Press, 1994).

[33] See William D. Edwards, Wesley J. Gabel, and Floyd E. Hosmer, "On the Physical Death of Jesus Christ," *The Journal of the American Medical Association* 255 (1986): 1455-63.

evidence and be fashioned around all the facts. As Philip Schaff put it, "The purpose of the historian is not to construct a history from preconceived notions and to adjust it to his own liking, but to reproduce it from the best evidence and to let it speak for itself."[34] We are left with no other explanation other than the fact that he rose from the dead. Alternative explanations are certainly possible, but if they are historical, they have to correspond to the evidence. The problem with the alternative explanations is they are not drawn from and do not fit all or any of the evidence.

A historian who smuggles in an assumption about what can or cannot happen in the course of human events—either by restricting explanations methodologically or by philosophical presuppositions—is not operating as a historian. They are confusing philosophical speculation with historical explanation. Ehrman's excursus is an example of exactly this. He rules out the possibility of a miracle like the resurrection by defining it as the most improbable event and restricting historians to consider only what he deems probable *apart* from consideration of the evidence. However, although a resurrection is not a normal human experience, the evidence is so compelling in the case of Jesus that the most probable explanation of the empty tomb is his resurrection. So not only can a historian explain the empty tomb by the resurrection. He or she is left with no real alternative but to assert what Christians confess: that Jesus was crucified under Pontius Pilate, died, was buried, and three days later rose again from the dead.

---

[34] Philip Schaff, *History of the Christian Church*, vol. 1 (New York: Charles Scribner's Sons, 1910), 175.

Natural Law: A Basis for Christian-Muslim Discourse?

It is often presumed—and rightly so—that the Law written on every human heart (Romans 2:14–15) provides a basis for Christian engagement in the secular realm. For one, it recognizes the existence of some common ground from which Christians can address moral issues in a pluralistic environment. It also provides a point of connection for evangelistic and apologetic efforts, for our innate sense of right and wrong and inability to consistently choose the former is a touchstone for articulating how at odds we are with the Author of the moral Law.[1]

For all its promise, though, working from natural law has its share of difficulties. This is particularly the case in a culture predominated by the assumptions of naturalism, a view of (at least knowable) reality being comprised of nature and only nature.[2] Without a supernatural author behind moral law, there can, upon analysis, be no real meaningful morality, only changing opinions guided by the shifting standards of culture.[3] This certainly impedes on evangelism,

---

[1] Robert Kolb, *Speaking the Gospel Today: A Theology for Evangelism* (St. Louis: Concordia, 1984), 42–43.

[2] See Phillip E. Johnson, "Darwinism as Dogma: The Establishment of Naturalism" and Nancy R. Pearcey, "Darwin Meets the Berenstain Bears: Evolution as a Total Worldview," in *Uncommon Dissent: Intellectuals Who Find Darwinism Unconvincing*, ed. William A. Dembski (Wilmington, DE: ISI Books, 2004), 23–40 and 53–73; Gary H. Locklair, "The Impact of Origin Paradigms on Culture," in *Christ and Culture in Dialogue*, ed. J. L. Menuge (St. Louis: Concordia, 1999), 220–38.

[3] See J. Budziszewski, *The Line through the Heart: Natural Law as Fact, Theory, and Sign of Contradiction* (Wilmington, DE: ISI Books, 2009), 79–95.

too, for consciences informed by naturalism yet convicted of failing to do what is right may experience guilt, but it will be interpreted as, at best, an imposition of culturally conditioned morality.[4]

That is the problem when the presumption of the natural law meets a naturalistic worldview. The latter presupposes a certain ontology that *a priori* denies metaphysical realities necessary for the existence of real natural law. But what about non-Christians who, while they may not confess the triune nature of God, believe in an objective moral law and transcendent moral lawgiver? Can a Christian carry on discourse with, for example, a Jew or a Muslim on the basis of some shared understanding of natural law? David Novak, a prolific conservative Jewish scholar, recently argued that certainly, with some qualification, Jews and Christians can. In fact, he contends that they must work together cooperatively in the realm of ethics, though he insists that Christians (and Jews) must, if they are to remain united in their joint ethical pursuits, resist attempts to use such discourses as venues for proselytizing.[5] (The Christian might agree, but would certainly look for opportunities and venues appropriate for evangelization.)

Interestingly, Novak also asks whether the same could be said of Islam and Muslims. He recognizes the difficulties presented by today's political climate, but he is optimistic about the possibility. There are progressive Muslim leaders, too, who would be quick to answer in the affirmative. For example, speaking of how Muslims might assimilate and contribute more in American society, Ingrid Mattson, president of the Islamic Society of North America (ISNA) and director of the MacDonald Center for the Study of Islam and Christian-Muslim Relations at Hartford Seminary, has argued that

---

However, also see the more rigorous critiques of those optimistic of discourse on the basis of natural law such as Carl F. H. Henry, "Natural Law and Nihilistic Culture," *First Things* (January 1995): 54–60; Daniel Heimbach, "Rethinking Natural Law: Is It Our Best Strategy for Engaging the Public Square?" *Liberty University Law Review* 2:3 (Spring 2008).

[4] For robust critiques of naturalism, see Stewart Goetz and Charles Taliaferro, *Naturalism* (Grand Rapids: Eerdmans, 2008) as well as Phillip E. Johnson, *Reason in the Balance: The Case against Naturalism in Science, Law & Education* (Downers Grove, IL: InterVarsity, 1995).

[5] David Novak, "Is Natural Law a Border Concept between Judaism and Christianity?" *Journal of Religious Ethics* 32:2 (2004): 249.

the "natural law tradition in Islam" needs to be recovered by Muslims for service in public moral discourse.[6] Russell Powell, a (Catholic) Christian and Associate Professor of Law at Seattle University School of Law, has gone so far as to argue that each tradition's understanding of natural law not only makes common moral pursuits such as social justice and human rights possible, but it could also promote reconciliation between the two faiths.[7] Alan Wisdom of the Institute on Religion & Democracy (IRD) is not so optimistic, but he has suggested that the motifs both religions hold in common may help illustrate "the 'natural law' or 'common grace' that is revealed to all, as Paul argues in Romans 1–2."[8]

This essay addresses the potential such an approach to Islam might hold. But before any assessment of the promise or perils can be achieved, the nature of Islam and, more specifically, natural law in Islam must be considered. Only then can the following question be addressed: Does natural law serve as an adequate basis from which Christians and Muslims can dialogue?

The Nature of Islam

To identify the nature of Islam is difficult, for it is and has been to some extent or another diversely interpreted and appropriated throughout its history. This is especially true with Muslims living in the West in the twenty-first century. If there is one way to characterize it, though, it would be to reject the tendency to view Islam as a religion.[9] It is more appropriately viewed as an ideology that, as ideologies do, purports to explain and seeks to inform (and ultimately legislate) every realm of human life. As the Muslim Student

---

[6] United States Institute of Peace, *Ijtihad: Reinterpreting Islamic Principles for the Twenty-first Century* (Washington, DC, 2004), 8.

[7] Russell Powell, "Toward Reconciliation in the Middle East: A Framework for Christian-Muslim Dialogue Using Natural Law Tradition," *Loyola University Chicago International Law Review* 2:1 (2004): 1–30.

[8] Alan Wisdom, "Christian-Muslim Dialogue: A Guide for Churches," *Institute on Religion and Democracy* (May 2003), http://www.theird.org/Page .aspx?pid=1082 (accessed January 29, 2010).

[9] For more on the nature of ideology, see Kenneth Minogue, *Alien Powers: The Pure Theory of Ideology* (Wilmington, DE: ISI Books, 2008), 5–6.

Association puts it, Islam is "the only true way of life.... The scope of this way of life is vast enough that it transcends the traditional notion of 'religion.' Islam includes submitting to Allah in the realm of politics, economics, law, etc."[10]

In a pluralistic environment one might expect Muslims to conceal or at least qualify this aspect of Islam. However, Muslim intellectuals are usually forthright about their totalizing vision for humanity. A leading Palestinian-American scholar in the previous century, Ismail al-Faruqi, for example, asserted that the principles of Islam and the subsequent culture it gave birth to "purports to speak for all humans and for all times."[11] More recently, Tariq Ramadan, one of the most influential yet controversial Western Muslim intellectuals, submitted that the principles advanced in the Qur'an as well as the example and assertions of Muhammad contained in biographies (*sira*) and collections of sayings and deeds of the so-called prophet (*hadith*) were "given for the universe...for all times and across all frontiers."[12]

It is in these sources that an ideology is advanced which is designed to be impressed upon human societies everywhere (using a variety of means) through a perpetual struggle (*jihad*) that will last until the Day of Judgment or up until the world confesses there is no god but Allah, and Muhammad is his messenger.[13] This struggle can take a variety of forms. Historically, it has been conceived, almost completely, as offensive political and military action. Currently, it is being carried out in a variety of other ways. The most obvious one is

---

[10] "Compendium of Muslim Texts," MSA West, http://www.msawest.net/islam/ (accessed January 29, 2010).

[11] Ismail al-Faruqi, "Islam and Culture and Civilization," in *Islam and Contemporary Society* (New York: Longman, 1982), 142.

[12] Tariq Ramadan, *Western Muslims and the Future of Islam* (New York: Oxford University Press, 2004), 63. For focused analyses of the Qur'an and the life and example of Muhammad, see Robert Spencer, *The Complete Infidel's Guide to the Koran* (Washington, DC: Regnery Press, 2009) and *The Truth of Muhammad: Founder of the World's Most Intolerant Religion* (Washington, DC: Regnery Press, 2007).

[13] Abu Dawud al-Sijistani, *Sunan Abu Dawud*, trans. Ahmad Hasan (Lahore: Ashraf Press, 1984), 2:702; Muhammad ibn Umar al-Waqidi, *Kitab al-Maghazi* (Oxford: Oxford University Press, 1966), 3:113.

terrorism. Some, however, have gone so far as to completely redefine jihad not as an outward struggle to advance the cause of Islam in society but an internal struggle with one's own temptation.[14] Probably the most notable form of jihad in the West (that is going virtually unnoticed) is what has been referred to as civilizational jihad, which seeks to supplant the values of Western society by presenting Islam as a legitimate and rational alternative.[15]

NATURAL LAW AND ISLAM

There is a rationale behind the efforts of Muslims to advance Islam in the West, and it is linked to the Islamic view of nature. To begin with, Muslims regard Islam as the religion of nature (*din al-fitrah*). In fact, the Qur'an "regards the whole universe as 'Muslim.'"[16] Everything in the heavens and earth, reads Qur'an 3:83, submits to its creator. That is, the design, order, and purpose of all of nature and creation are but a reflection of its submission to the laws of nature and, behind them, their author, Allah. While the universe and all its parts operate in accordance with these divinely written laws, there is one exception—humankind.

Unlike the rest of creation, humans have free will (albeit ultimately limited by God's will) and are therefore capable of disobedience. This is not to suggest the Qur'an teaches that humans have an inherently sinful disposition. Quite the contrary; Islam decries the biblical doctrine of original sin and advances a very different anthropology. The term usually associated with it is *fitrah*. Linguistically,

---

[14] David Cook has demonstrated this reformulation, when characterized as the essential nature of historical jihad, to be completely false and misleading. See his *Understanding Jihad* (Berkeley: University of California Press, 2005).

[15] Mohamed Akram, "An Explanatory Memorandum on the General Strategic Goal for the Brotherhood in North America" (May 1991), http://www.investigativeproject.org/document/id/20 (accessed February 1, 2010). On jihad in America generally, see Steven Emerson, *Jihad Incorporated: A Guide to Militant Islam in US* (Amherst: Prometheus Books, 2006); Robert Spencer, *Stealth Jihad: How Radical Islam is Subverting America without Guns or Bombs* (Washington, DC: Regnery Publishing, 2008).

[16] Fazlur Rahman, *Major Themes of the Qur'an* (Chicago: University of Chicago Press, 2009), 65.

it refers to the inborn natural disposition of things. As a theological anthropological concept, it refers to the inherent righteousness or, at the very least, morally neutral essence of human beings. What is more, though, is that *fitrah* also refers to the status of the natural human, who has yet to go through various circumstances in life (nationality, family, etc.) and be seduced away from Islam, as being a Muslim since and even before birth. Qur'an 7:172 says that even before the creation of Adam, all of humankind was in some way raised into existence, and a covenant was established between Allah and humankind where-upon all humankind, so that they would be without excuse on the last day, testified that Allah was their Lord.

This passage "provides the best introduction to the Islamic understanding of humans' relations with God," writes Hartford Seminary's Yahya Michot. Allah "is the creator of everything...Whose decree none of His creatures is able to escape. We are God's [Allah's] slaves, totally subjugated...to God's [Allah's] creative will, decision, and power."[17] If the nature of human beings is understood this way— as those born in a state of submission and owned by Allah—then it is easy to see why, or at least understand the rationale behind, the drive in Islam to struggle, as Qur'an 9:33 puts it, to cause Islam to prevail over all other systems of belief. For if the whole universe is Muslim and humans have even made a covenant with Allah himself, and yet they go their own way by constructing their own religious, political, and domestic institutions, this would represent the height of arrogance, disobedience, and rebellion, leading to universal chaos and ignorance.

The resulting ignorance from the rebellion of humankind is one of the reasons Allah enjoined Muslims to fight and advance the cause of Islam (Qur'an 2:216). It is also the reason, the Qur'an teaches, that Allah once raised up prophets—beginning with Adam through Abraham, Moses, David, Jesus, and terminating with Muhammad— so that people in former times might turn to Allah and his law. The words of the prophets in Islam are not necessarily viewed as special

---

[17] Yahya Michot, "The Image of God in Humanity from a Muslim Perspective," in *Abraham's Children: Jews, Christians, and Muslims in Conversation*, ed. Norman Solomon, Richard Harries, and Tim Winter (London: T & T Clark, 2006), 167–68.

revelation, though. Rather, the prophets told the people what they could know for themselves by reflecting upon nature. "The primary task of the prophets is to awaken man's conscience so that he can decipher the primordial writing on his heart more clearly and with greater conviction."[18] It is only because the "abundant revelation in nature has by itself mostly failed to elicit the appropriate response from human beings" that God sent prophets. But when Muhammad, the seal of the prophetic revelation, died in 632, the duty to "ensure that [Islam] is everywhere recognized" has now been passed onto the global Muslim community.[19]

The motif of Islam being the religion as well as the divinely created law of nature and, moreover, that it is available to those that search deep and hard enough is quite prominent in the Qur'an. In fact, one of the greatest American Muslim scholars of the last century asserted that the Qur'an regards Allah's law as being "written upon man's heart."[20] Yet, scholars have shown that historically and even contemporaneously the prevalent view suggests "humans could not have an inner moral compass, or any 'law written on their hearts' (Romans 2:15), enabling them to live moral lives on the basis of their own unaided reason."[21] This has, in fact, led to a peculiar view that all "knowledge, any 'science' in Islam, as well as the initiative and the ways to practice it, must be derived from the Holy Qur'an, the Word of God, and from hadith, the reports of the sayings of the Prophet of Islam."[22]

There is logic to this, too. It is, as one scholar explains, "because there is always the possibility that reason may lose sight of the limits imposed on her as an instrument of knowledge and mistake herself for both the chief subject and object, not only the sources of

---

[18] Rahman, *Major Themes of the Qur'an*, 24.

[19] Daniel A. Madigan, "Themes and Topics," in *The Cambridge Companion to the Qur'an*, ed. Jane Dammen McAuliffe (New York: Cambridge University Press, 2006), 84-85, 94.

[20] Rahman, *Major Themes of the Qur'an*, 24.

[21] Patricia Crone, *God's Rule: Government and Islam* (New York: Columbia University Press, 2004), 263–64.

[22] Steffen A. J. Stelzer, "Ethics," in *The Cambridge Companion to Classical Islamic Theology*, ed. Tim Winter (New York: Cambridge University Press, 2008), 161.

knowledge but also the procedures of knowing must be formulated on the ground of divine and prophetic authority. In other words, reason may not always be able to determine by herself whether she 'follows reason.'"[23] Reason and nature are not the most trustworthy sources of spiritual or ethical insight, for they will always be potentially misused and misinterpreted by humans. Thus, the view that "there was no better way of speaking about God—and therefore no better theology—than quoting what God Himself says about Himself in the Qur'an" has largely prevailed in classical Muslim thought.[24]

But there has always been a rationalist school of Islamic thought, and it seems to be gaining ascendancy.[25] Contemporary Muslim scholars, particularly those working in or at least attempting to influence Islam in the West, are resurrecting what seems to be a new emphasis on reason and natural law. One such example is Ali Ezzati's unique book, *Islam and Natural Law*.[26] After a brief excurse on the origins of natural law theory in Greco-Roman thought, its appropriation by medieval Christian theologians, and eventual decline, neglect, and rejection in modern Western intellectual history, Ezzati concludes his first chapter on natural law in the West by drawing attention to its revival in the last quarter of the twentieth century. Then in subsequent chapters he details its place in Islam, as if to proffer it (Islamic ideology) as a viable alternative to the morass of Western relativistic pluralism.

---

[23] Stelzer, "Ethics," 162.

[24] Yahya Michot, "Revelation," in *Cambridge Companion to Classical Islamic Theology*, 190. See, for example, A. Kevin Reinhart, *Before Revelation: The Boundaries of Muslim Moral Thought* (Albany: SUNY Press, 1995), 70–75. Cf. with Robert R. Reilly's fascinating thesis entitled *The Closing of the Muslim Mind: How Intellectual Suicide Created the Modern Islamist Crisis* (Wilmington, DE: ISI Books, 2010).

[25] For an historical study of the rationalism or, as it is often called, mu'tazilism in Islam, see Richard Martin, *Defenders of Reason in Islam: From Medieval School to Modern Symbol* (Oxford: Oneworld Publications, 1997).

[26] Ali Ezzati, *Islam and Natural Law* (London: Islamic College for Advanced Studies Press, 2002). For a scholarly historical study of natural law in the Islamic tradition, see Anver M. Emon's "Natural Law and Natural Rights in Islamic Law," *Journal of Law and Religion* 20:2 (2004–2005): 351–95 and, more recently, *Islamic Natural Law Theories* (New York: Oxford University Press, 2010).

Ezzati is clearly confident of the primacy of natural law in Islam. Islam teaches, he writes,

> its adherents that God [Allah] created nature and implanted therein its laws, orders and ends. It commanded man to discover these in order to enable him to enjoy nature as God [Allah] has entitled him to do. Islam suggests that God [Allah] has created everything in nature perfect. He has fashioned each creature and given it an essence, a structure that determines its life and from which it never deviates. He has placed every creature and all parts of nature within the general nexus of nature so that its birth, its whole life and its death all happen according to patterns which are themselves constituents of the divine will. To every creature He has ordained a career and objective to which its existence is forever subject. There is no gap or conflict in nature. No object or event in nature is an accident. Everything that is or happens does so because of predictable cause and with predictable consequences. That is why nature is real cosmos, not a chaos where events never take place with cause, or sometimes with and sometimes without cause.[27]

As such, Ezzati can describe Islam as both "natural" and "rational."[28] This, he argues, is the way it has been regarded throughout the classical age; any descriptions of it as being nonrational are misinterpretations (perhaps even willful misinterpretations) of history. In fact, Ezzati argues that if there is a major religious tradition hostile to reason and natural law, it would be Christianity since at least the time of the Reformation.[29]

To advance a principle or position on something as natural (that it corresponds to what one finds in nature) and rational (that it is internally coherent) implies that it is objective. And if something is objective, it means that, at least in principle, rational persons reflecting on the world outside of themselves will draw similar (if not the same) conclusions. Ezzati makes this exact claim for Islam.

Basically, two different religions and ethical systems exist, he argues. One is the religion of nature, "*din al-fitrah* or *religio naturalis*,

---

[27] Ezzati, *Islam and Natural Law*, 74–75.

[28] Ezzati, *Islam and Natural Law*, 72.

[29] Ezzati, *Islam and Natural Law*, 29ff., 186–87.

which any human being possesses by birth." The other is historical religion or the "religious traditions of history." By this, Ezzati means those religions that have developed in and are a product of historical processes. They may be "outgrowths of *din al-fitrah*." Yet, in varying degrees they are "accumulations, figurations, interpretations or transformations of history," the product or inventions of "time, place, culture, leadership and other particular conditions." Christianity and the ethics that spring from it, and all other religions, fall within this category. They may have elements of truth within them insofar as they agree with natural religion, but they are still not commensurate with the natural religion. Islam, however, is, for in quintessentially circular logic, Ezzati states, "Islam calls this *din al-fitrah* or Ur-religion, 'Islam.'"[30]

Even more interesting are the claims Ezzati makes for the objectivity of Islamic law and ethics. Both are the heart of Islam. The former may be more fundamental than the latter, but the two are inseparable and comprise the essential makeup and character of Islam.[31] Ultimately, the source of Islamic law (*shariʻah*) is the Qurʼan and the multitude of traditions related to Muhammad (contained in biographies and orally transmitted anecdotes), but analogical reasoning and the consensus of the Muslim community also play a determinative role for issues not explicitly addressed in the foundational texts.[32] And even though drawn from texts written in a particular language at a certain point in history, Islamic law (and ethics) is still regarded as comprehensive and universal. It is designed as legislation for all people and for every aspect of their individual and collective behavior—from domestic to international relations and everything in between—for it is seen not as the law of human beings, but Allah's law for humanity. And just as the theology of Islam is proffered not only in texts but also in nature, the same could be said for Islamic law. There is, Ezzati maintains, perfect harmony between Islamic law and

---

[30]   Ezzati, *Islam and Natural Law*, 62.

[31]   See A. Kevin Reinhart, "Islamic Law as Islamic Ethics," *Journal of Religious Ethics* 11:2 (1983): 186–203.

[32]   For an introduction to the theory of Islamic law, see Mohammad Hashim Kamali, *Shariʻa Law: An Introduction* (Oxford: Oneworld Publications, 2008), and for an historical overview, see Knut S. Vikør, *Between God and the Sultan: A History of Islamic Law* (New York: Oxford University Press, 2005).

reason and the ethical principles it finds in nature.[33] In light of this, Ezzati expects that human beings who think rationally about nature and its laws will draw the same conclusions of traditional Islamic law and ethics.

This is the overall thrust of Ezzati's book (and contemporary Islamic rationalism), but his ambitious volume serves even a larger purpose. He advances a clandestine apologetic for Islam within it. His central argument is that the West is mired in ethical relativism, which is largely because the Western mind is no longer anchored in any sort of metaphysic. While Christianity once provided one, Western society has distanced itself from its historical intellectual roots and, conversely, Christianity has distanced itself from rationality and nature. In Ezzati's estimation, the only way to resolve the resulting relativism on the one hand and irrationalism on the other is through Islamic rationalism. Not only can Islamic rationalism help one navigate the secular realm,[34] employing reason and studying nature the way even a non-Muslim would, but Muslims can rest assured that its rational pursuits will yield the result of Islam.

CHRISTIAN—MUSLIM DISCOURSE

The presumption that natural law provides a basis for Christian discourse with others in the domain of ethics is reasonable. This is particularly true when it comes to discourse with those who hold nature and its laws as the work of a creator. Thus, it must be maintained that there is always the possibility for Christians to engage in reasoned discourse with Muslims. Such discourse may even be fruitful, if not necessary, in the secular realm, as David Novak has argued, to combat the ethical relativism legitimized by the ideology of secularism.[35]

---

[33] Ezzati, *Islam and Natural Law*, 88–89.

[34] On this theme, see Abdullah Ahmed an-Na'im, *Islam and the Secular State: Negotiating the Future of Shari'a* (Cambridge: Harvard University Press, 2008).

[35] Novak, "Is Natural Law a Border Concept between Judaism and Christianity?" 252. One should, however, be aware of the fact that it is a fairly standard polemic to blame Christianity and its distinction between the sacred and secular realm for the rise of secularism. See, for example, Syed Muhammad Naquib al-Attas, *Islam, Secularism and the Philosophy of the Future* (New York:

But one must be realistic. Islam is an ideology, and ideologies ultimately do not allow for rational neutrality. Any shared ethical principles derived from reflection upon nature will, in the end, be interpreted by a Muslim in light of Islamic law. Or at least the expectation is that the findings of reason will conform to the principles proffered in the Qur'an and traditions of Muhammad. One should also be aware of the way any sort of conceived consensus between Christians and Muslims is used to advance the cause of Islam. The Qur'an endorses such an approach.[36] In fact, Christians in particular are singled out as being the closest potential friends of Muslims, but only because they are potential converts.[37]

One conspicuous example of the awkward results of Christian–Muslim discourse was the Common Word initiative.[38] It began in the fall of 2007 when 138 influential Muslims came together in Jordan under the auspices of the Royal Aal al-Bayt Institute for Islamic Thought and produced a document entitled "A Common Word between Us and You." Afterward, this document was sent to the pope, patriarchs, archbishops, presidents, and general secretaries of Christian church bodies everywhere. It asserted that for the purpose of peace Christians and Muslims, who collectively make up over half of the world's population, must work together, for "our common future is at stake." And in view of this, it concluded by urging Christians, on the basis of the common ethical motifs they share with Muslims, to work with Muslims "in righteousness and good work... and live in sincere peace, harmony and mutual goodwill."[39]

The response from Christians was overwhelming. Yale University's Center for Faith and Culture, for example, immediately

---

Mansell, 1985), esp. 13–46; Sayyid Qutb, *Islam: The Religion of the Future* (Riyadh: International Islamic Federation of Student Organizations, 1984), esp. 34–60.

[36] See, for example, Qur'an 3:64–73.

[37] See, for example, Qur'an 5:82–83.

[38] See http://www.acommonword.com and Miroslav Volf, Ghazi bin Muhammad, and Melissa Yarrington, eds., *A Common Word: Muslims and Christians on Loving God and Neighbor Together* (Grand Rapids: Eerdmans, 2010).

[39] "A Common Word between Us and You," http://www.acommonword.com /index.php?lang=en&page=option1 (accessed May 30, 2010).

drafted "Loving God and Neighbor Together: A Christian Response to *A Common Word between Us and You*," and published it, affixed with the signatures of 300 prominent Christian scholars and clergy, in the *New York Times* on November 18, 2007.[40] In their desire to extend a hand of friendship to the Muslim world, the respondents ultimately, but presumably unwittingly, acknowledged the legitimacy of Islam. Even a cursory read of the response from the Yale Center for Faith and Culture made it clear that the authors (and signatories) presumed nature's creator to be both the God of Islam and Christianity,[41] named Muhammad as a prophet, and made other desperate concessions (such as implicating contemporary Christians in the medieval Crusades and apologizing for excesses in the war on terror, as if it were a new crusade instigated and led by Christians). The letter from Yale wasn't anomalous either, for since the fall of 2007 there have been innumerable appeasements made by Christian leaders from every tradition.[42]

Despite the dubious nature of common initiatives advanced under the guise of Christian–Muslim dialogue, there is still room for discourse. Only such discourse, if it is truly to be natural law discourse, will not be Christian–Muslim discourse. It will be discourse between humans reflecting on the innate knowledge of right and wrong as well as moral principles reflected in nature. There will always be trouble, however, when such findings are absorbed or appropriated into a previously existing set of beliefs such as Islamic law. Islam cannot help itself, though, for it is ideological and legal in nature, whereas Christianity is chiefly concerned with the status of the human before God, and, while there may be ethics peculiar to

---

[40] "Loving God and Neighbor Together: A Christian Response to *A Common Word between Us and You*," http://www.yale.edu/faith/acw/acw.htm (accessed May 20, 2010).

[41] On this, see Timothy George, *Is the Father of Jesus the God of Muhammad* (Grand Rapids: Zondervan, 2002).

[42] For analyses and critiques of the Common Word initiative, which unsurprisingly get no media attention, see Jochen Katz, "A Common Word between Us and You: Evaluating the Muslim Open Letter," http://www.answering -islam.org/Letters/common_word.htm (accessed February 20, 2010); Sam Solomon and E. al-Maqdisi, *A Common Word: The Undermining of the Church* (Charlottesville: Advancing Native Missions, 2009).

Christians, Christianity is largely comfortable with law being inter-preted and implemented by any just legislator.

So while Christians strive to "live peaceably with all" (Romans 12:18), including Muslims, we would be wise to proceed cautiously in joining with Islam in a common cause in any regard. In fact, a cursory examination of Islam and its final view of Christianity reveals that, under certain circumstances, Muslims are enjoined to fight Christians until they willingly embrace Islam or compulsorily submit to Islamic governance and law (Qur'an 9:29). Being aware of this and a host of other issues is essential for any serious discourse with people who describe themselves as Muslim.

Still, it is equally necessary that Christians avail themselves to Muslims, as difficult as it may seem, for the sake of the Gospel; for though their assumptions may tell them differently, Muslims stand before God by nature sinful and unclean and, like us, in desperate need of a Savior. Since Islam has no Savior, a strong proclamation of Law and Gospel and the ability to give an apologia for criticisms and questions that arise are the Christian's best dialogue and evangelistic tools. The Holy Spirit still works through the Word to convict sinners of their sin and bring them to repentance and saving faith.

The Relevance of Islamic Theology

Islam is and will continue to be one of Christianity's greatest challenges.[1] Certainly there are other pressing issues. Regardless of how one prioritizes them, though, Islam will—or at least should—remain high on the list. The reasons for this are multi-faceted. Demographics, economics, and geopolitics all play a significant part,[2] but for all the problems they raise, there is a deeper one that is only beginning to rear its ugly head: its theology.

This may sound extravagant or alarmist, but consider this: Islam is being marketed as a peaceful inclusive religion that is underpinned by a natural and rational theology. And, moreover, it is increasingly asserting itself as a corrective to the excesses and innovations introduced into Christianity. Very recently, Muslim apologists have been citing Western scholarship—from Walter Bauer's *Orthodoxy and Heresy in Earliest Christianity* to Bart Ehrman's *Misquoting Jesus*—to back up these claims. Hence, as Abdul Saleeb puts it, "Muslims... feel a great sense of intellectual justification for their rejection of orthodox Christianity. They can point to the fact that the theological challenges that they have brought against Christianity for most

---

[1] C. George Fry, "The Witness of the Cross and the Islamic Crescent," in *The Theology of the Cross for the 21st Century: Signposts for a Multicultural Witness*, eds. Alberto L. Garcia and A.R. Victor Raj (St. Louis: CPH, 2002), 83-102.

[2] See, for example, Mark Steyn's *America Alone: The End of the World as We Know It* (Washington D.C.: Regnery Publishing, 2006). One will, however, want to compare his provocative argument with Philip Jenkins's *God's Continent: Christianity, Islam, and Europe's Religious Crisis* (New York: Oxford University Press, 2007) as well as Richard John Neuhaus's "The Much Exaggerated Death of Europe," *First Things* 173 (May 2007): 32-38.

of their history have been echoed by Western liberal tradition in biblical studies for at least the past two hundred years."[3]

It is rather imperative, then, in preparing for inevitable encounters with Islam, to be acquainted with its underlying theology. Failure to do so, wrote Robert W. Yarbrough, "is a strategic error," for it will guarantee a wholly inadequate and, at best, flaccid response on the part of Christians as they face a "religious future to some extent already with us." Yarbrough adds, writing nearly two decades ago, that this future may be "one which may see an attempt to reduplicate the Arab conquests of the seventh and eighth centuries."[4]

Recent events suggest Yarbrough's words were almost prescient. This is not to suggest that there is currently an organized attempt on the part of some sovereign Muslim state—equal to the burgeoning Arab empire of the four caliphs (632-661) and Umayyads (661-750) in the seventh and eighth centuries—to overrun America. There are certainly violent non-state actors—Al-Qaeda being the most notorious—who have this as a long-term goal.[5] And there are also other actors within the United States itself who seek, through non-violent and even civil means, the gradual Islamization of America.[6] But the point is this: Islam and its theology are with us to stay.

---

[3] Abdul Saleeb, "Islam," in *To Everyone an Answer: A Case for the Christian Worldview*, ed. Francis J. Beckwith et al. (Downers Grove: IVP, 2004), 354. Cf. Saleeb (with R.C. Sproul), *The Dark Side of Islam* (Wheaton: Crossway Books, 2003), 9-14. For recent examples, see especially the work of Louay Fatoohi: *The Mystery of the Historical Jesus* (Birmingham: Luna Plena, 2007) and *The Mystery of the Crucifixion* (Birmingham: Luna Plena, 2008). For the historical origins and early precedents of this relatively new turn in Muslim apologetic strategies, see Christine Schirrmacher's *Mit den Waffen des Gegners, Christlich-Muslimische Kontroversen im 19. und 20. Jahrhundert, dargestellt am Beispiel der Auseinandersetzung um Karl Gottlieb Pfanders 'mîzân al-haqq' und Rahmatullâh ibn Khalîl al-'Uthmânî al-Kairânawîs 'izhâr al-haqq' und der Diskussion über das Barnabasevangelium* (Berlin: K. Schwarz Verlag, 1992).

[4] Robert W. Yarbrough, "New Testament Christology and the Jesus of Islam," *Evangelical Review of Theology* 14 (1990): 125.

[5] See especially Steven Emerson, *Jihad Incorporated: A Guide to Militant Islam in the US* (Amherst: Prometheus Books, 2006).

[6] See Robert Spencer, *Stealth Jihad: How Radical Islam is Subverting America without Guns or Bombs* (Washington, DC: Regnery Publishing, 2008).

Demographic facts alone indicate this. Just twenty years ago in 1990, when Yarbrough urged Christian awareness with Islamic theology, there were about 500 million Muslims in the world. Today, there are over 1.3 billion scattered across the globe. In the United States, where there were 30 mosques less than twenty years ago, there are now over 2,000. Just to the north of us, in Canada, there are now more Muslim teenagers than there are Protestants. In light of all this, the theology of Islam must be taken seriously, for it has, whether we like it or not, become extremely relevant.

So what is Islam? The term itself is derived from the Arabic root, *salam*, and literally means submission to Allah, the eternal, uncreated, and singular (in essence and in person) creator (Qur'an 112:1-4). A person or entity in a state of submission or obedience to him is, according to the participle form of *salam*, a Muslim. While these terms do not appear in the historical record until the seventh century,[7] Muslims do not see their religion as one born in seventh-century Arabia. It is not conceived of, as most encyclopedic descriptions put it, as the youngest of the monotheistic religions. Muslims believe that Islam—a religious disposition characterized by submission to the creator—has existed from the beginning of creation.

In fact, it is often described as a natural religion.[8] For Muslims it is *the* natural religion (*din al-fitrah*)—the religion that was woven by Allah into creation. The influential Muslim ideologue Sayyid Abul Ala Maududi (1903-1979) boldly claimed that all of nature bore witness to this fact. He wrote:

Everyone can see that the universe we live in is an orderly universe. There is law and order among all the units that comprise this universe.

---

[7] Some historians have noted that the terms "Islam" and "Muslim" cannot be found in any text until a century-and-a-half after Muhammad's death. This indicates, at least for the revisionists, that the traditional narrative (perhaps the Qur'an itself) may have been, and was probably to some degree or another, invented after the Arab conquest of Syria, Palestine, and North Africa. See, for example, Yehuda D. Nevo and Judith Koren, *Crossroads to Islam: The Origins of the Arab Religion and the Arab State* (Amherst: Prometheus Press, 2003).

[8] See, for example, Abdul Wahid Hamid, *Islam: The Natural Way* (Chicago: Kazi Publications, 2004).

Everything is assigned a place in a grand scheme which is working in a magnificent and superb way....

This powerful, all-pervasive law, which governs all that comprises the universe, from the tiniest specks of dust to the magnificent galaxies in high heavens, is the law of God, the Creator and Ruler of the universe. As the entire creation obeys the law of God, the whole universe, therefore literally follows the religion of Islam—for Islam signifies nothing but obedience and submission to Allah, the Lord of the universe.[9]

This is precisely what the Qur'an claims. Allah reveals himself through evidences or signs (*ayat*), which, in addition to testifying to his existence, "manifest all we need to know about God and about our rightful place in relationship to God."[10]

Islam's chief concern, then, is the submission of human beings to Allah. The problem with human beings is that, unlike the rest of creation, men and women have a limited free will. Most of creation, perforce, submits to the laws of the universe, and therefore submits to God. Humans, however, have "been given freedom of thought, choice, and action,"[11] but for whatever reasons, despite the "abundant revelation in nature," the signs of God have by themselves "mostly failed to elicit the appropriate response from human beings."[12] This is not the result of a depraved moral state inherent in humanity, for there is no concept of original sin in Islam.[13]

But there is a fall; only it is a literal fall from heaven to earth. The story goes as follows. During Allah's act of creating the cosmos, which occurred over the course of six days (Qur'an 7:54), a row emerged

---

[9] Sayyid Abul Ala Maududi, *Towards Understanding Islam*, 22nd ed. (Lahore: Idara Tarjuman-ul-Quran Ltd., 1995), 2-3.

[10] Daniel A. Madigan, "Themes and Topics," in *The Cambridge Companion to the Qur'an*, ed. Jane Dammen McAuliffe (New York: Cambridge University Press, 2006), 83. For a thorough treatment of this theme, see Annemarie Schimmel, *Deciphering the Signs of God: A Phenomenological Approach to Islam* (Albany: State University of New York Press, 1994).

[11] Maududi, *Towards Understanding Islam*, 4.

[12] Madigan, "Themes and Topics," 84.

[13] George Anawati, "La Notion de 'Péché Originel' existe-t-elle dans l'Islam?" *Studia Islamica* 31 (1970): 29-40; Johan Bouman, *Gott und Mensch im Koran* (Darmstadt: Wissenschaftliche Buchgesellschaft, 1977).

after he informed the angels of his intention to create humankind as his representative authority—his *khalifa* (from which the term caliph is derived)—on earth. The angels questioned the wisdom of this, and asked him why he would hand over his authority to humans knowing they would, by virtue of their free will coupled with their fallibility, be prone to corruption and the shedding of blood. But Allah's mind was made up, and his response to the angels was curt: "I know that which you do not know" (2:30).

Allah vested humanity with more than earthly authority, though. He also commanded that the angels bow down before Adam and Eve. The angels (who have no volition in Islam) followed Allah's decree, although they did not like it. But a jinn (a bodiless creature with free will), who had been welcomed in the company of angels, rebelled, arguing that he should be considered of higher stature than human beings (7:11-12). The jinn's name was Iblis. After his fall from Allah's favor, he was given the title of Satan, but not before Allah described him as the one who would work to deceive humanity (17:61-65).

And deceive humanity he would. The Qur'an explains that, after the creation of Adam and Eve, Allah placed them in a garden, and forbade them from one thing: eating the fruit from a certain tree. But Satan began to entice them, telling them the only reason Allah forbade them from eating from it was because he wanted to keep them from becoming immortal like the angels. Trusting in the lies of Satan, rather than Allah, they ate and "brought about their fall." Afterwards, Allah confronted Adam and Eve, asking them why they fell to the temptation of Satan. The couple responded, "Our Lord, we have wronged ourselves. If you do not forgive us or grant us mercy, we will be lost." Allah countered, saying, "Get down from here.... You will dwell on earth... There you will live, die, and be raised" (17:19-25).

There is an implicit promise of eternal life here. Adam and Eve were told that, even though they had disobeyed Allah, they would, along with their descendants, be raised from the dead. How will this be accomplished? Allah explains, after the literal fall from paradise down to earth (not a fall into sin): "restraint from evil" (17:26).

To enlighten human minds, keep them from falling into evil, and dissuade them from infidelity, the Qur'an teaches that Allah has sent prophets and messengers to warn humankind of the consequences of such unfaithfulness and to clarify the signs of Allah in nature. The first of these prophets was Adam. After being expelled from the garden, Allah absolved and revealed to him what the Qur'an calls "guidance" (2:37-38). "This guidance," explains Tariq Ramadan, "is the series of Revelations that came throughout human history."[14] It provides the requisite information one needs to submit wholly to Allah, thereby overcoming evil.

One of the key motifs of Islamic prophetology is the belief that the message of Islam has been transmitted from the time of Adam through Abraham, Moses, David, Jesus, and a whole host of other prophets up until the time of Muhammad. Each was called to confirm and complete the message of the previous prophet and, if it had been tampered with, to correct and restore it to its pure state.

The Qur'an's message, it must be stressed, is not that there are three successive monotheistic religions—Judaism, Christianity, and then Islam—but that every prophet preached the same religion throughout the history of humanity. Thus, according to Islam, Muhammad merely "renewed the teachings of Adam, Noah, Moses, Aaron, [and] Jesus" while, at the same time, giving "further detail to them."[15] Thus, one of the most influential classical Muslim scholars, Ibn Taymiyya, wrote in his polemic against Christianity, *Al-Jawab al-Sahih*, "Muslims are those who follow the religion of Christ, Moses, Abraham, and the rest of the messengers."[16] Christianity and Judaism are seen, in traditional Muslim theology, not as legitimate theological predecessors but as theological deviations of Islam.[17]

---

[14] Tariq Ramadan, *Western Muslims and the Future of Islam* (New York: Oxford University Press, 2004), 202.

[15] F.E. Peters (ed.), *A Reader on Classical Islam* (Princeton: Princeton University Press, 1994), 160. Muslim theologians make a distinction between religion (*din*) and law (*sharia*), whereas the religion of the prophets is one the divine law changes over time in accordance with the context in which it is revealed. On this, see Maududi, *Towards Understanding Islam*, 142-143; Kenneth Cragg, *Jesus and the Muslim: An Exploration* (London: George Allen and Unwin, 1985), 17-74.

[16] Thomas F. Michel (ed. and trans.), *A Muslim Theologian's Response to Christianity: Ibn Taymiyya's Al-Jawab al-Sahih* (Delmar, NY: Caravan Books, 1985), 249.

[17] See Muhammad Azizan Sabjan and Noor Shakirah Mat Akhir, "The Misconception of the Revealed Religion," *The Islamic Quarterly* 52 (2008): 65-78.

This theme of a continuous and perpetual theology passed down through the prophets is prominent in the Qur'an. It even ascribes to some of these prophets books, books that are, at least in name, familiar to us. For example, Qur'an 3:3-4 reads: "It is he who has sent down the Book [the Qur'an] to you with truth, confirming what came before it. And he sent down the Torah and the Gospel, beforehand, as guidance for mankind."

The content of this passage in addition to others addressing the relationship of the Qur'an to the Judeo-Christian Scriptures has forced Muslim apologists to develop theories accounting for the differences, as a natural reading of the quranic text endorses the Gospel and Torah as revelations from Allah. One view asserts that the Torah and Gospel are essentially lost books and are not identical to the Torah and Gospel of the Old and New Testaments. A second theory advances the position that the Qur'an confirms what is in the Torah and the Gospel, but alleges that Jews and Christians have derived unnatural meanings from the text. For example, Deuteronomy 18:18 has, they claim, been falsely attributed to Jesus when, in fact, it refers to Muhammad, as does the promise of the paraclete in the gospel of John. The third and most popular theory is that the Torah and Gospel have been textually altered.[18]

Had they not been, they would have taught the core content of Muslim doctrine. A passage from the Qur'an said to sum this up reads: "He is Allah, the one necessary being. He begets not; nor was he begotten, and there is none equal or comparable to him" (112:1-4). This unitarian doctrine of God—known as *tawhid*—is more than just a general profession of monotheism, though. To understand Islam and its view of God, one needs to understand not just what the doctrine of *tawhid* asserts, but also what it rejects. The Muslim doctrine of God asserts that Allah is one, and, while in the act of creation he revealed himself, he is not associated with creation in any way. We might call this transcendent monotheism, but the god of Islam is not

---

[18] For the issue of the "corruption" (*tahrif*) of the Bible, see Joseph M. Mutei, "The Bible: Classical and Contemporary Muslim Attitudes and Exegesis," *Evangelical Review of Theology* 31 (2007): 207-220; Abdullah Saleeb, "The Charge of Distortion of Jewish and Christian Scriptures," *Muslim World* 92 (2002): 419-436.

like the watchmaker of the Enlightenment deists, who, after endowing creation with laws to sustain it, left it on its own. Rather, he reveals himself especially in the Qur'an not in temporal or mutable words, but in speech spoken from all eternity. It is in the inscripturation of his word—and only there—that Allah becomes immanent in the spatio-temporal world.

This explains the extreme reverence Muslims have for the Qur'an. It also explains Islam's disdain for the doctrine of the incarnation. Not only does Allah "not beget," but it is impossible, according to Qur'an 6:100-101 and other similar passages (e.g., 19:35, 92; 72:3), for him to have a son because he has no female consort. It concludes that such an assertion, that Christ was and is the son of God or the word of God incarnate, according to Qur'an 19:89, is irrational and "a terrible evil thing" and, moreover, damnable (9:30).

This blatant rejection of the cornerstone of Christian theology originates in the Qur'an's warning to avoid *shirk*. *Shirk* is the failure to maintain the absolute oneness, transcendence, and inimitability of Allah by attributing partners or associates to him. For example, polytheism, as *shirk* is often rendered in English, is perhaps the crassest form. However, included in the list of those guilty of ascribing partners to God—called *mushrikun*—are Christians who say that Jesus is the son of God. The Qur'an thus warns Christians:

> O people of the book do not exceed the limits in your religion, nor speak anything of Allah except what is true. Jesus the messiah, the son of Mary, was no more than a messenger of Allah…. Believe in Allah and his Messengers. Do not confess, "God is triune!" Cease! It will be better for you, for Allah is one God; he is far too exalted to have a son (4:171).

When Muhammad pronounced this in seventh-century Arabia, this warning had not just theological but also political implications. The Muslim forces were (and perhaps are still) instructed to "kill the *mushrikun*"—that is, those guilty of *shirk*—"wherever you find them, and capture them and besiege them, and lie in wait for them in an ambush" (9:5) And the "final ruling" on how the Muslim community was (and is) to relate to Christianity (and Judaism) is to struggle against them not until they converted to Islam—for as Qur'an 2:256

says there is no compulsion in religion—but until they submit to Islamic rule and law.[19]

This struggle (*jihad*) to advance the cause of Islam is found throughout the Qur'an. It is a religious and moral obligation. "Fighting has been prescribed for you," reads Qur'an 2:216. It is not a temporal injunction either; Qur'an 8:39, 9:5 and 29 make it clear that Christians, Jews, and other non-Muslims are to be fought "until there is no more division and all religion is for Allah."

This was, according to one of the earliest historical sources on the emergence of Islam, the mission of Muhammad. In the final sermon that he delivered to the first generation of Muslims, he announced that he had been commanded by Allah to make war against all people until they acknowledged that there was no god but Allah.[20] This is certainly how the growth of Islam was accomplished in the seventh and eighth centuries. It also provided the impetus for further imperial expansion later on.[21] And it still remains a religious obligation today.

It may not always take a physically aggressive form; it can take the form of theological polemics and apologetics, political activism, or cultural intrusions. Whatever its form, its goal is the advancement of Islam.[22] There will be no end to this struggle, either; "the jihad," Muhammad claimed (and Islamic jurisprudence affirms), "will remain perpetual until the day of judgment."[23]

The blatant political agenda of Islam should make it clear that this is not simply a religion, especially as religion is conceived of in the post-Enlightenment and postmodern West. It is an all-encompassing worldview and political theology through which Muslims

---

[19] Sayyid Qutb, *In the Shade of the Qur'an: Fī Zilāl al-Qur'an,* vol. 9, trans. and ed. Adil Salahi (Leichestershire: The Islamic Foundation, 2003), 101-102.

[20] Muhammad ibn Umar al-Waqidi, *Kitab al-Maghazi* (Oxford: Oxford University Press, 1966), 3:113.

[21] See Efraim Karsh, *Islamic Imperialism: A History* (New Haven: Yale University Press, 2006); Andrew Bostom, *The Legacy of Jihad: Islamic Holy War and the Fate of Non-Muslims* (Amherst: Prometheus Press, 2005).

[22] The best scholarly source on jihad is David Cook's *Understanding Jihad* (Berkeley: University of California Press, 2005).

[23] Abu Dawud al-Sijistani, *Sunan Abu Dawud,* trans. Ahmad Hasan (Lahore: Ashraf Press, 1984), 2:702. Cf. Mohammad Hashim Kamali, *Principles of Islamic Jurisprudence,* third ed. (Cambridge: Islamic Texts Society, 2003), 207.

see the world as composed of two spheres—the sphere of Islam (*dar al-Islam*) and the sphere of war (*dar al-harb*). The sphere of Islam is the geographical space in which governments and legal system are at least informed by but, according to most, based solely on the Qur'an and tradition.[24] The sphere of war comprises the non-Muslim territories, especially areas where Muslims "are neither protected nor able to live in peace."[25] Although there is, in classical Islamic thought, some grey area, for the majority of Muslims today and throughout history, the world is and has been viewed through this bipolar lens.[26]

Tariq Ramadan argues that this "does not necessarily mean that a state of war exists between the opposing 'abodes.'"[27] That may be true if one takes into account the wide array of classic Muslim texts on the subject. However, if Muslims are to bring about political and legal changes—even when it is not pursued by physical force but within existing political and legal structures—it does mean that there is and will be, in some way or another, "permanent conflict" or, at the very least, ideological and theological encounters of some sort between Islam and the world.[28]

This is what one would expect from a universal ideology designed for the world, to restore the world to its original order.[29] The interesting thing in all this is that while Muslim organizations dress up Islam in modern Western clothes, most are clear about its universal designs. The Muslim Student Association, for example, explains Islam as "the only true way of life revealed from the Creator. The scope of this way of life is vast enough that it transcends the traditional notion of

---

[24] See Patricia Crone, *God's Rule: Government and Islam* (New York: Columbia University Press, 2000).
[25] See Ramadan, *Western Muslims*, 65. Also see Yahya Michot, *Muslims under Non-Muslim Rule* (Oxford: Interface Publications, 2006).
[26] Ramadan has called for Muslims to rethink this tradition (*Western Muslims*, 62-101).
[27] Ramadan, *Western Muslims*, 65.
[28] Karsh, *Islamic Imperialism*, 63-83.
[29] The only way to avoid this, according to the Muslim scholar Bassam Tibi, is for the depoliticizing of Islam. See his *Islam between Culture and Politics* (New York: Palgrave Macmillan, 2001). One could argue, however, that Islam depoliticized is not Islam.

'religion.' Islam includes submitting to Allah in the realm of politics, economics, law, etc."[30] Even Ramadan, often heralded as the great Western Muslim innovator, asserts that the theological principles given in the Qur'an and other sacred traditions of Islam (such as the *hadith*) were "given for the universe...for all times and across all frontiers."[31] This means that they are applicable for Christians in America, too, and it is time that it be exposed and, in due time and with careful preparation, encountered.

---

[30] http://www.msawest.net/islam/
[31] Ramadan, *Western Muslims*, 63.

Jesus, Muslims, and the Gospel

There are several revisionist theories regarding the origins of Christianity peddled in popular academic culture. One of the more pervasive ones claims that a number of legitimate yet competing understandings of Jesus existed in the first century. Some viewed him as a great moral teacher. Others saw him as a political activist. Still others considered him an apocalyptic preacher. At some point, the theory goes, men began to attribute a divine nature to him. And in order to achieve ecclesial and political hegemony they established this as the orthodox position.

This thesis is asserted in a variety of contemporary sources such as the various works of the Jesus Seminar, popular historical fictions like Dan Brown's *Da Vinci Code,* and the scholarship of Bart Ehrman and Elaine Pagels. But it is not all that new. It was, in fact, proposed back in 1934 by the German scholar Walter Bauer (1877-1960) in *Orthodoxy and Heresy in Earliest Christianity.*

Long before Bauer, however, apologists for Islam advanced similar arguments. For example, one of the most formidable and influential Muslim theologians, Taqi al-Din Ahmad ibn Taymiyya (1263-1328), argued that the original understanding of Jesus and Jesus' understanding of himself was that he was merely a human prophet of Allah. Orthodox Christian Christology was a later development. Therefore, he concluded in the voluminous *Correct Response to those who Corrupted the Religion of the Messiah*, the "false religion of Christians is nothing but an innovated religion which they invented after the time of Christ."[1]

---

[1] Thomas Michel, *A Muslim Theologian's Response to Christianity: Ibn Taymiyya's* Al-Jawab Al-Sahih (Delmar: Caravan Books, 1984), 143.

It is tempting not to take such claims seriously. But consider this: contemporary Muslim literature on Jesus is increasingly asserting that Islamic Christology is supported by modern historical and biblical scholarship. The work of Louay Fatoohi, an Iraqi-born Christian who converted to Islam while attending university in Britain, is perhaps the most recent example. In *Mystery of the Historical Jesus* (2007) he draws upon the scholarship of Bauer, Ehrman, and several others, and argues that a critical examination of primary historical sources necessarily leads one to the conclusion that the Jesus of the Qur'an is the real historical Jesus.

A number of other sources advancing similar claims—from books to youtubeislam.com—have Muslims convinced that Western biblical scholarship has vindicated the claims of Islam.[2] Some, such as *What Did Jesus Really Say?*, go so far as to suggest that, on account of current historical research on Jesus, "the most learned among the Christian community are slowly recognizing the truth and drawing closer to Islam."[3]

This, it seems, is reason enough to take seriously the Muslim understanding of Jesus. But there are others. Demographically, Islam has experienced exponential growth over the last century. Around 1906 America's "apostle to Islam," Samuel Zwemer (1867-1952), estimated that there were about 200 million Muslims across the globe. Today, the number is around 1.3 billion. And while the Muslim population in America is notoriously difficult to assess—with figures ranging from 2 to 10 million—one thing is clear. The number of mosques scattered across the country has skyrocketed. In just 1990 there were about thirty. In 2001, there were over 1200. Today, it is estimated that there are over 2000.

Socio-cultural and attendant political challenges notwithstanding, this presents a unique opportunity for Christian outreach. In decades past, Christians had to travel overseas to find major Muslim populations where it was (and still is) illegal (and punishable by death) to proselytize to them. Now, many Muslims who come from countries

---

[2] See Abdul Saleeb (with R.C. Sproul), *The Dark Side of Islam* (Wheaton: Crossway, 2003), 9-14.

[3] Misha'al ibn Abdullah, *What Did Jesus Really Say?* (Ann Arbor: Islamic Assembly of North America, 1996), 66.

with such restrictions live next door, attend schools, and work with us. In light of this, the possibilities for Muslim encounters with the gospel of Jesus Christ are and will continue to be an ever-increasing reality. Before addressing the issues surrounding such an encounter, though, a brief assessment of the Muslim understanding of Jesus is in order.

THE MUSLIM JESUS

Jesus figures prominently in the theological narrative of Islam. He was one of the 124,000 prophets Allah raised up long before the time of Muhammad, the last of the prophets, to provide ethico-religious and legal guidance for the nations of the world. Among these prophets, though, he stands out, with Moses, David, and Muhammad, as a messenger who also recorded Allah's word in a book, called the *Injil* or (as it is commonly translated) Gospel.

The Qur'an depicts Jesus, in some cases, not entirely unlike the canonical gospels. For example, Gabriel's annunciation of the birth of a son to a virgin named Mary is recounted. She is also described as being related to Zechariah who, despite his wife's old age, was promised a son later named John (the Baptist).

The Qur'an does not, however, give the geographical or geopolitical details of Jesus' birth. There is, for example, no report of a census issued by Caesar Augustus at the time that Quirinius was governor of Syria. Neither does it record the trip from Nazareth to Bethlehem with Joseph or the birth of Jesus in a manger.

Instead, it provides an ambiguous and contradictory description of Jesus' nativity. It explains that, after Jesus' conception, Mary withdrew to a remote place to hide her pregnancy. Eventually, she gave birth under a palm tree, and immediately thereafter—to comfort his distraught mother—Jesus spoke his first words, directing his mother to a stream of fresh water and some dates for refreshment. Afterwards, when Mary returned to her kin with a newborn child, she was not disgraced, for the infant Jesus explained how it was not through adultery but Allah's miraculous intervention that she gave birth. "I am a servant of Allah," the child Jesus declared, "He has given me the Scripture and made me a prophet!" (Qur'an 9:16-33).

There are other miracles attributed to Jesus in the Qur'an. Chapter 5:110 surmises that, in addition to speaking from the cradle, he was also able to breathe life into a bird made of clay, heal the blind and leprous, and raise people from the dead. But none of these should be understood as a product of his divine powers. They were nothing but miracles of Allah designed to bear witness to his prophetic vocation.

The Qur'an is quite clear that the Jesus described in its pages was nothing more than a human messenger of Allah. He was created by Allah in Mary's womb, and although given the honorific title of Messiah and even referred to as the word of Allah, it warns against attributing any divine properties to him.

> Do not commit excess in your religion or say about Allah anything but the truth. Jesus the Messiah, the son of Mary, was only a messenger of Allah.... Allah is but one God. Exalted is he above having a son (Qur'an 4:171).

In fact, those who do attribute divine sonship to Jesus are guilty of the most heinous and unforgivable sin of *shirk*. Such a profession is so serious that Muhammad called upon Allah to destroy such people and enjoined Muslims to bring them into submission through physical force as they carry out the timeless struggle to "cause Islam to prevail over all other religions" (Qur'an 9:29-33).

This irreconcilable difference with the biblical teaching on the person of Jesus is further complicated by the Qur'an's different picture of Jesus' mission. Islamic theology insists that Jesus and the Gospel was sent to confirm that which was revealed in the Torah before it, as well as to provide ideational and legal guidance to his contemporaries, and finally to announce and prepare humankind for the arrival of the last of Allah's prophets.

Jesus, son of Mary, said, "O Tribe of Israel, surely I am the messenger of Allah to you, confirming what was revealed before me in the Torah, and bringing good news of a messenger who will come after me, whose name is Ahmad" (Qur'an 61:6).

Ahmad is another name for Muhammad, and Muslim apologists insist that this passage is simply a reiteration of John 14:16. They therefore contend that the helper or comforter in the biblical text refers not to the Holy Spirit but to Muhammad.

These sorts of arguments and the Qur'an's general endorsement of the Gospel of Jesus raise some interesting problems. The Qur'an claims in a variety of places that the Gospel confirms the Torah and anticipates the Qur'an. Allah sent the Qur'an down to Muhammad, "confirming what came before it, and he sent down the Torah and the Gospel before this" (Qur'an 3:3). The issue that plagues Muslim apologists, then, is: Why is it that the Gospel and the Qur'an, particularly, teach very contradictory theologies and have different versions of what they both purport to be real empirical history?

One of the most popular traditions asserts that the original Gospel of Jesus has been lost. Matthew, Mark, Luke, and John are erroneous redactions of the original. Some deviously suggest that the Gospel of Barnabas—a forgery probably inspired by a convert to Islam dating to no earlier than the fourteenth century—is the closest to the original source that we have. Other Muslim apologists argue that the text of one, some, or all of the canonical gospels, at the time of their composition, were accurate renditions of the Gospel spoken of in the Qur'an. But, they continue, that Christians have over the centuries altered the actual text. Still others claim that the text is basically sound. It is only the interpretation of it that is not. All in all, they claim that either the canonical texts or the interpretation of it has been forced into a Procrustean bed of a later theology that divinized a human prophet named Jesus.

Along with its condemnation of the confession of the deity of Christ, the Qur'an has no room for the doctrine of the atonement. "Every soul draws its own merits; no one can bear the burdens of another" (Qur'an 6:164). Therefore, every human being will be judged on the basis of their own deeds. But the Christian doctrine of atonement is not just theologically incorrect; it makes no historical sense either, for the Qur'an declares that Jesus was not crucified; nor did he die (4:157). Instead, he was raised up unto heaven where he awaits his final return on judgment day. At that time, the Qur'an says, he will turn his back on those who considered him divine.

CHRISTIANS AND MUSLIMS

It is here—particularly the denial of the crucifixion of Jesus—that Islam poses one of its greatest challenges to Christianity. And Muslims know it! In a widely circulated book entitled *Crucifixion or Cruci-fiction?* Ahmed Deedat asserted (with reference to 1 Corinthians 15:14), "If

Jesus did NOT die, and he was NOT resurrected from the dead, there can be NO salvation in Christianity!... In a nutshell, No Crucifixion!— No Christianity!"[4]

This presents a major dilemma to Christian evangelism of Muslims, for without the cross of Christ (and, of course, the resurrection) there is no evangel. This, Islam's rejection of the reliability of the canonical Gospels, and the perception that Muslims are tough nuts to crack, has led many missiologists to emphasize the friendship approach to Muslims. And there is much to be said for this approach. It is indeed vital to establish a good rapport with Muslims.

At some point, however, Muslims need to hear the gospel of the historical and biblical Jesus. Certainly, a sinful and fallen will sets up insurmountable barriers that the Holy Spirit alone, working through a clear articulation of the gospel, can penetrate. But there are some (pseudo) factual barriers that must be brought down, too. The most conspicuous is, of course, the misunderstanding of the person and work of Jesus.

One could approach this in a number of ways. But a concentrated apologetic will start with the very issue of the crucifixion and death of Jesus. The strength of this method is that it can—at least initially—avoid sticky theological issues![5] The question of whether Jesus died on a cross around AD 30 just outside of Jerusalem is at its most basic level an historical one. And there are a host of first-century literary sources testifying to it. There are eyewitnesses (such as Matthew and John), companions of eyewitnesses (such as Mark and Luke), and several non-Christian accounts reporting the crucifixion and death of Jesus as a brute historical fact (e.g., the Roman and Jewish historians [respectively] Tacitus [56-120] and Josephus [37-100], Talmudic literature, the Syrian stoic Mara Bar Serapion [fl. 73], and the Greek satirist Lucian of Samosata [120-180]).[6]

---

[4] Ahmed Deedat, *Crucifixion or Cruci-Fiction?* (Woodside, NY: Islamic Propagation Center International, n.d.), 2.

[5] A good apologetics text for dealing with theological issues is Norman Geisler's and Abdul Saleeb's *Answering Islam: The Crescent in Light of the Cross* (Grand Rapids: Baker, 2002).

[6] See, among a host of others, F.F. Bruce, *Jesus and Christian Origins outside the New Testament* (Grand Rapids: Eerdmans, 1974).

There is no good historical reason to prefer the Qur'an on the matter of Jesus' death—a seventh-century document (at best)—over the testimony of eyewitnesses and first- and second-century writers.[7] In fact, a wide array of liberals, skeptics, and atheists agree, in John Dominic Crossan's words, that Jesus' crucifixion "is as sure as anything historical ever can be."[8]

The resurrection of Jesus, too, can be shown to be an historical fact.[9] But a detailed argument may or may not be necessary.[10] If one can show the Qur'an to be untrustworthy on at least one aspect of the life of Jesus, it should very well prompt further questions about who he really was. The Christian should and must be prepared to address these questions. But the best strategy is simply to insist upon sticking with the primary sources for Jesus' life and mission.

The goal should be to get Matthew, Mark, Luke, or John into the hands of Muslims. There they will see—from the testimony of those who were in the best position to tell us about Jesus—just who Jesus was and what he did. Friendship, acts of kindness, and genuine hospitality goes a long way in fostering the right environment for effective evangelism. But it is the testimony of the Gospel writers that provides the most reliable witness to the gospel.

---

[7] Although Louay Fatoohi has recently tried to suggest this in *The Mystery of the Crucifixion: The Attempt to Kill Jesus in the Qur'an, the New Testament, and Historical Sources* (Birmingham: Luna Plena, 2008).

[8] See Lee Strobel, *The Case for the Real Jesus* (Grand Rapids: Zondervan, 2007), 113-114.

[9] To see how one might advance this point vis-à-vis a Muslim, see Michael Licona, *Paul Meets Muhammad: A Christian-Muslim Debate on the Resurrection* (Grand Rapids: Baker, 2006).

[10] Interestingly, some Muslims (mostly those in marginal sects within Islam) have accepted Jesus' crucifixion but not his death. See, for example, Hadhrat Mirza Ghulam Ahmad's outrageous *Jesus in India: Jesus' Deliverance from the Cross and Journey to India* (Gurdaspur: Islam International Publications, 2003). Also see the debate over the death and resurrection between John Warwick Montgomery and Shabir Ally available in audio format: http://www.ciltpp.com/tap_deba.htm.

The Challenge of the New Atheism

The year 2004 was, for many reasons, an interesting year in the history of atheism. Rumors that Antony Flew, the world's most notorious atheist, was beginning to rethink his position were confirmed when he publically announced he had become a theist. Explaining himself, he wrote:

> [C]onsistent with the principle I have embraced since the beginning of my philosophical life—of following the argument no matter where it leads...the journey to my discovery of the Divine has thus far been a pilgrimage of reason. I have followed the argument where it has led me. And it has led me to accept the existence of a self-existent, immutable, immaterial, omnipotent, and omniscient Being.[1]

In the same year, Alister McGrath published *The Twilight of Atheism* wherein he traced the emergence, eventual scientific vindication, and then political legitimization of atheism from the late eighteenth until the twentieth centuries, but concluded that the seeming intellectual respectability of hardboiled atheism had probably run its course. Its metaphysical assumptions had been exposed and intolerance criticized and challenged by the new, as he put it, "cultural mood" of postmodernism.[2] In fact, McGrath argues that,

---

[1] *There Is a God: How the World's Most Notorious Atheist Changed His Mind* (New York: HarperCollins, 2007), 75, 155. Also see "My Pilgrimage from Atheism to Theism: A Discussion between Antony Flew and Gary Habermas," *Philosophia Christi* 6/2 (2004): 197-211.

[2] Alister McGrath, *The Twilight of Atheism: The Rise and Fall of Disbelief in the Modern World* (New York: Doubleday, 2004), 227.

while acknowledging that many postmodern philosophers are atheists, "postmodernity...does not for one moment imply or entail that
there is no God. Postmodernity affirms a philosophical modesty, noting limits to our knowledge; it does not—and, indeed, cannot—make
declarations concerning what exists and what does not exist." In fact,
he continues, "postmodernity seriously undermines the plausibility
of atheism."[3]

McGrath seemed to confirm what many Christian postmodern
thinkers had been and still are saying: atheism and modernist epistemology have lost their influence and control over Western society.
It is no longer the case, as Lesslie Newbigin described it in the mid
1980s, that Western society "is—in its public philosophy—atheist."[4]
The alleged tolerance indicative of postmodernity has opened all sorts
of promising opportunities for the Christian church to express and
assert itself without fear of reprisal from the atheistic forces of modernity.[5] The way this works out, per the suggestions of some authors,
is that Christians will no longer need to bother with giving a defense
of the faith. For all intents and purposes, Christianity is absolved of
the apologetic task, at least the way it was defined in modernity.[6]
But while everyone was jumping on board the trendy postmodern
bandwagon, almost out of nowhere, shortly after Flew announced
his "conversion" and McGrath argued that strident atheism had been
discredited, a book was published that seems to have changed the

---

[3] McGrath, *The Twilight of Atheism*, 227. This does not necessarily imply
postmodernism offers promise to Christianity. See Richard John Neuhaus, "Can
Atheists Be Good Citizens?" *First Things* 15 (Aug-Sept 1991): 17-21; Charlotte
Allen, "Believe It," *National Review* 56:17 (2004): 51-52.

[4] Lesslie Newbigin, *Foolishness to the Greeks: The Gospel and Western
Culture* (Grand Rapids: Eerdmans, 1986), 65.

[5] For a taste of the intolerance of at least one postmodern thinker, see
Richard Rorty, "Universality and Truth," in *Rorty and His Critics*, ed. Robert
B. Brandom (Oxford: Blackwell, 2000), 21-22.

[6] See, for example, Philip D. Kenneson, "There's No Such Thing as Objective
Truth, and It's a Good Thing, Too," in *Christian Apologetics in the Postmodern
World*, eds. Timothy R. Phillips and Dennis L. Okholm (Downers Grove:
IVP, 1995), 155-170; James K.A. Smith, *Who's Afraid of Postmodernism:
Taking Derrida, Lyotard, and Foucault to Church* (Grand Rapids: Baker
Academic, 2006).

intellectual environment. Its title was *The End of Faith*, authored by a then PhD student in neuroscience named Sam Harris. The book immediately climbed to number four on the *New York Times* bestseller list and has been followed by a whole slew of volumes similar in spirit and unified in their agenda. A few examples include Richard Dawkins's *The God Delusion*; Daniel C. Dennett's *Breaking the Spell: Religion as a Natural Phenomenon*; Victor J. Stenger's *God, The Failed Hypothesis*; and Christopher Hitchens's, *God Is Not Great*. All these books (and many more) argue for the dominance of atheism as a worldview and the marginalization, if not eradication, of religion. And far from being abstract philosophical treatises for the intelligentsia, they were written for mass consumption. Their influence and the impact of their arguments have effectively ushered in—in just a few years—what has been termed the "new atheist movement."[7]

WHAT IS THE "NEW ATHEISM"?

It is hard to define the new atheism with any sort of precision. Victor Stenger—himself a neoatheist—describes it as a "militant, in-your-face kind of atheism," one which, with the exception of Madalyn Murray O'Hair and her ilk, had fallen out of fashion during the late twentieth century.[8] Others have characterized it as evangelical, for its chief personalities are overt in their intention to advance the atheist cause. Richard Dawkins, for example, wrote in the preface to *The God Delusion*, "If this book works as I intend, religious readers who open it will be atheists when they put it down."[9] More than a few of the new atheists could be described as ideological and totalitarian. Sam Harris, for instance, has suggested some religious beliefs are "so dangerous that it may even be ethical to kill people for believing them."[10] This sentiment, considered alongside his acceptance of the prospect of a "world government,"[11] is eerily reminiscent of the

---

[7] Victor J. Stenger, *The New Atheism: Taking a Stand for Science and Reason* (Amherst: Prometheus Books, 2009), 27.

[8] Viktor Stenger, *The New Atheism: Taking a Stand for Science and Reason* (Buffalo: Prometheus Press, 2009), 25.

[9] Richard Dawkins, *The God Delusion* (New York: Mariner Books, 2008), 5.

[10] Harris, *The End of Faith*, 52-53.

[11] Harris, *The End of Faith*, 151.

totalizing vision of international communism and its supporting philosophy of dialectical materialism. But other neoatheists could be described as liberal secularists. Christopher Hitchens, for example, falls somewhere between neoconservatism and classical liberalism. Christian conservative talk show host Hugh Hewitt, in fact, intimated, while introducing him at Biola University that, despite their differences, Hitchens was still an ally in championing political liberty.

Where the neoatheists seem totally united—and one of the defining features of the movement—is in their espousal of what could be termed scientism, a view that asserts natural science is the only way to understand the cosmos. This is often informed by an ontological assumption, memorably expressed by Carl Sagan: that the cosmos is all there was, is, and ever will be. In other words, they begin with the presumption of materialism. Ockham's razor or the principle of parsimony, they argue, demands that we 1) view the universe as all that there is because "thanks to the telescope and the microscope"—the tools of natural science—it is no longer necessary to appeal beyond or before it to explain the universe and life within it.[12]

So how do the new atheists explain the origins or existence of the universe and the complexity of life on earth? Looking at the latter first (because they are more certain and much more unified on this), they could all be described fairly as ultra-Darwinian fundamentalists.[13] So firm and ideological in nature is their commitment that Daniel C. Dennett, a decade before neoatheism emerged, suggested that anyone who even questions "that the variety of life on this planet was produced by the process of evolution [via the mechanism of natural selection] is simply ignorant—inexcusably ignorant."[14] And those incapable of passively accepting macro-level biological evolution across species as a fact should be quarantined.[15] In his most recent book, *The Greatest Show on Earth*, Dawkins has argued that "the 'theory' of [macro-] evolution is actually a fact—as incontrovertible

---

[12] See Hitchens, *God is Not Great*, 70, 282.

[13] The term is derived from Stephen Jay Gould's "Evolution: The Pleasures of Pluralism," *New York Review of Books* 44 (1997): 47.

[14] Dennett, *Darwin's Dangerous Idea*, 46.

[15] Dennett, *Darwin's Dangerous Idea*, 519.

a fact as any in science."[16] Parents who resist it being taught as such in their children's schools are guilty of intellectual child abuse. As such, advancing Darwinian evolutionism is central on the agenda of the new atheism.

Darwin's theory, by their own admission, only purports to explain the mechanism and general process of biological evolution. It does not explain where or how life originated. The new atheists are somewhat agnostic on this issue, with one exception. They will entertain theories such as directed panspermia (which supposes life came to earth either, as Michael Ruse put it in Ben Stein's *Expelled*, on the backs of crystals or, as Richard Dawkins suggested, through the agency of some sort of extraterrestrial intelligence). But what they will not entertain—even as a working hypothesis—is the agency of a supernatural deity.

The same goes for their explanation of the existence of the universe. Victor J. Stenger, author of *God, the Failed Hypothesis: How Science Shows that God Does Not Exist*, wrote a paper recently addressing that perennial cosmological question: Why is there something rather than nothing? This is, and has been, a major philosophical problem. It's especially a problem for the materialist atheist. Not to fret, though, science has a possible solution according to Stenger. And here it is: "Another universe existed prior to ours that tunneled through the unphysical region…to become our universe."[17] To be sure, Stenger does note the lack of any empirical evidence for such a theory. But he is quick to add that standards in contemporary physics and cosmology do not rule it out. Therefore, he assumes such a scenario must not only be plausible but because it appeals only to natural causation, it or some other naturalistic model is the only conceivable one.[18]

This dogmatic naturalism or materialism is the worldview to which the new atheists are committed. To be fair, they occasionally do argue that this is not an all-encompassing ontological assumption.

---

[16] Dawkins, *The Greatest Show on Earth*, vii.

[17] Victor J. Stenger, "A Scenario for a Natural Origin of Our Universe Using a Mathematical Model Based on Established Physics and Cosmology," *Philo* 9 (2006): 100.

[18] For a brief but sufficient critique, see Berlinski, *The Devil's Delusion: Atheism and Its Scientific Pretensions* (New York: Crown Forum, 2008), 97.

Rather, it is the conclusion they have drawn based upon a total consideration of the evidence. Knowing, however, that much of the same evidence and the same universe to which they appeal to validate their materialism are also used by others to vindicate theistic realism, much of the work of the new atheists is directed at refuting classical theistic arguments.

One of the standard and classical proofs for God's existence is the cosmological argument. It can be stated a number of ways. Perhaps the most lucid (and compelling) contemporary formulation is William Lane Craig's Kalām Cosmological Argument, which reads:

1. Whatever begins to exist has a cause.
2. The universe began to exist.
3. Therefore, the universe has a cause.[19]

Craig then argues that "from the very nature of the case, as the cause of space and time, this supernatural cause must be an uncaused, changeless, timeless, and immaterial being which created the universe.... It must be timeless and therefore changeless...because it created time. Because it also created space, it must transcend space as well and therefore be immaterial, not physical."[20] Interestingly, the new atheists don't address this version, but instead prefer to attack historical versions, completely ignoring the philosophical milieu in which it was composed. For example, Richard Dawkins, going back to Thomas Aquinas in the thirteenth century, renders the cosmological argument: "There must have been a time when no physical things existed. But, since physical things exist now, there must have been something non-physical to bring them into existence, and that something we call God."[21] Then he complains that this argument all depends upon the impossibility of an infinite regress. Thus, to "invoke God to terminate it" is arbitrary, he argues. It is, instead, more in line with the principle of parsimony to posit a natural cause

---

[19] For an extensive rendering of the argument, see William Lane Craig, *The Kalām Cosmological Argument* (New York: The Macmillan Press, 1979).

[20] See William Lane Craig and Walter Sinnott-Armstrong, *God? A Debate between a Christian and an Atheist* (New York: Oxford University Press, 2004), 5.

[21] Dawkins, *The God Delusion*, 77.

such as "a 'big bang singularity', or some physical concept as yet unknown."[22]

Dawkin's argument is weak on several levels. First, it is anachronistic. Of course it presumes the impossibility of an infinite regress. This was part and parcel of the medieval philosophical milieu. Such a presumption, however, has been demonstrated reasonable and veritable by contemporary science, too.[23] Secondly, if Dawkins does not like God as an explanation for why there is something rather than nothing, he must supply a more reasonable one. This he does not do. Appealing to a "big bang singularity" still begs the question of causation. Likewise, suggesting we must wait for a "physical" or material explanation is a cop-out, and it also betrays his assumptions. That a material explanation must be supplied presumes that that is the only explanation. *A priori* ruling out an immaterial and transcendental being seems just as presumptuous and perhaps even more so than presuming the impossibility of an infinite regress.

Another major argument for God's existence the new atheists spend a great deal of time refuting is the argument from design to a designer. The various ways it is formulated today is quite potent; in fact, Antony Flew credits it with his newfound philosophical theism. Nevertheless, Richard Dawkins and others who follow his argument purport to deal it a death blow.[24] The positive argument proposes that the best explanation for the apparent design of the universe and biological organisms within it is the existence of a designer. To the contrary, Dawkins argues that, while scientists still await an adequate explanation for cosmological design, biological evolution by the blind process of natural selection is a better explanation. Why? Because, he argues, a divine designer requires further explanation. Never mind that he acknowledges the materialist has yet to have an explanation for the fine-tuning of the universe. And that the probability of a living organism generating from nothing and then, regardless of how much time is allowed, evolving upwards from simple to

---

[22] Dawkins, *The God Delusion*, 77-78.

[23] David Hilbert, "On the Infinite," in *Philosophy of Mathematics*, second ed., ed. Paul Benacerraf and Hillary Putnam (New York: Cambridge University Press, 1983), 183-201.

[24] See Dawkins, *The God Delusion*, 157-158.

complex has never been observed and is genetically impossible. If a divine designer is the best or most reasonable inference, it does not necessarily need further explanation, but positing the mathematically and scientifically impossible does. It is for this reason that what Dawkins calls "a very serious argument against God's existence" has recently been labeled "the worse atheistic argument in the history of Western thought."[25]

One of the most interesting arguments in the polemics of neo-atheism is its take on the moral argument. The argument can be stated numerous ways. In its most basic form, though, it asserts that the only way to account either for an objective sense of morality or the universal and transcendental nature of moral obligations is the existence of a divine moral lawgiver. Otherwise, the only other plausible option is moral relativism. Interestingly, the new atheists acknowledge this and ultimately posit the latter. And then they explain the objective feeling and transcendental appearance of morality as just another aspect of our evolution. Dawkins writes that the only reason most human beings strive to behave morally, particularly around other human beings, as if there is an objective and transcendental standard of morality, is not because there is a real immutable natural moral law. Instead, he claims morality has simply evolved either because of our "genetic kinship," the anticipation of reciprocity for a moral favor, or the evolutionary benefit of having a reputation for being generous and kind.[26]

The new atheists have also used the issue of morality to advance a polemic against religion, particularly Christianity. Knowing, sensing, or perhaps just anticipating the accusation that once morality and ethics are torn from their metaphysical anchor, all standards of morality will disappear, they skirt the issue and point away from the epistemic and ontological problems of atheist morality to the moral atrocities committed in the name of religion. All the new atheists take great delight in citing historical instances of theologically-inspired violence—the crusades, the inquisition, the Salem witch trials, the mass suicide down in Jonestown, the Sarin gas attacks in Tokyo by

---

[25] See also William Lane Craig, "Dawkins's Delusion," in *Contending with Christianity's Critics: Answering New Atheists & Other Objectors*, ed. Paul Copan and William Lane Craig (Nashville: B&H Academic, 2009), 2-5.

[26] Dawkins, *The God Delusion*, 219.

Aum Shinrikyo, and of course the events of September 11, 2001. All of these travesties were carried out by people who believe in God. Thus, they argue, historical facts prove that religion or belief in God doesn't necessarily inspire moral behavior.

Sam Harris goes further, though, claiming that people of faith are actually the most dangerous people on earth. He writes, "Whenever a man imagines that he need only believe the truth of a proposition, without evidence…he becomes capable of anything."[27] It is therefore time we recognize that, he asserts, "all reasonable men and women have a common enemy. It is an enemy so near to us, and so deceptive, that we keep its counsel even as it threatens to destroy the very possibility of human happiness. Our enemy is nothing other than faith itself."[28]

In view of this, one might wonder: Is it not a fact that atheist political regimes—and not Christian ones—are responsible for most of the bloodshed of the twentieth century? Is it not the case that the total of all deaths caused by atheist regimes far outnumber those motivated by religion? In fact, yes. Researchers estimate that below 300,000 people were killed during the Crusades, Inquisition, and Salem witch trials, the three chief episodes neoatheists like to cite as indicative of what happens when Christian theology informs domestic and foreign political policy. R.J. Rummel's *Death by Government* reports that atheistic communism led to the murder (or, as he calls it, democide) of 110 million people. Add the atrocities legitimized by German national socialism to that and the number increases several million more. Now, no one really wants to get into the blame game, but it certainly is interesting how the new atheists respond to this. Harris argues that, while it is true that anti-religious regimes are responsible for the unprecedented violence of the twentieth century, they were not rational anti-religious atheistic regimes. They were, in fact, delusional regimes infatuated less with reason "than with race, economics, national identity, the march of history, or the moral dangers of intellectualism."[29] The neoatheists and their agenda represent rational atheism, of course. Moreover, Harris claims that much of the violence and bloodshed in Europe during the twentieth century

---

[27] Harris, *The End of Faith*, 85.
[28] Harris, *The End of Faith*, 131.
[29] Harris, *The End of Faith*, 231.

was in fact rooted in its Christian history.[30] The Holocaust is a case in point. According to Harris, the "anti-Semitism that built the crematoria brick by brick—and that still thrives today—comes to us by way of Christian theology."[31]

This sort of polemic indictment is standard fare in the new atheist literature. All of it warns about the dark days ahead if religion is not eradicated, but, at the same time, evinces a bit of optimism. For example, Hitchens ends *God Is Not Great* by rallying his readers to the new atheist cause, the renewal of the Enlightenment and new rational civilization. "However," he concludes, "only the most naïve utopian can believe that this new human civilization will develop, like some dream of 'progress,' in a straight line. We have first to transcend our prehistory, and escape the gnarled hand which reaches out to drag us back to the catacombs and the reeking altars and the guilty pleasures of subjection and abjection…. To clear the mind for this project, it has become necessary to know the enemy, and to prepare to fight it."[32] Daniel Dennett expresses things less pugnaciously but just as assertively in *Breaking the Spell* when he recommends that school—and not just science—curriculum be informed and guided by philosophical materialism. Belief in God and religion in general leads to ignorance. Atheism leads to enlightenment, and counting on the victory of an atheistic worldview inculcated in schools, he writes, "It will be fascinating to see what institutions and projects our children will devise…to carry us [guided by atheistic humanism] all safely into the future."[33] Harris likewise concludes *The End of Faith* similarly, noting that the success but also the survival of human civilization depends on whether or not religion and faith are marginalized and their legitimacy rejected. His and other new atheists' fears are that if religion continues to be legitimized, it will be increasingly politicized and will play a part in informing secular politics, leading to what the late Harvard political scientist Samuel Huntington called a clash of civilizations. He projected back in the 90s that the shape of future conflict would by driven primarily by the underlying theology or

---

[30] Also see, Dawkins, *The God Delusion*, around 278.
[31] Sam Harris, *The End of Faith*, 79.
[32] Hitchens, *God Is Not Great*, 283.
[33] Dennett, *Breaking the Spell*, 339.

worldview of the world's civilizations. The only solution and source of hope, then, in Harris's words, are seeing the "days of our religious identities" as "numbered. Whether the days of civilization itself are numbered would seem to depend, rather too much, on how soon we realize this."[34] It is this last sentiment that really drives the new atheists. Harris, Hitchens, Dawkins, and Dennett sometimes even designate themselves the four horsemen of the counter apocalypse. The seemingly altruistic concern for humanity—as simplistic, naïve and even sappy as it seems—is what boosts their credibility, too.

What impact has it had?

It would be hard to measure in any meaningful way how much of an impact the new atheists have actually had. It's too new of a movement. But what evidence we do have suggests it has experienced quite a bit of success. Not only have the key figures of the movement published bestsellers, indicating they are at least being widely read, but they are also influencing high school and college students. Atheist and agnostic student groups are popping up all over the country alongside the ones that already exist.

In addition to this rather practical local concern, however, the new atheists have been largely successful in reintroducing some of the same arguments and debates of modernity. It might, then, behoove us to ask what impact it has, or at least should have, upon Christians, particularly those in environments where atheism thrives. I think it is obvious that, at the very least, the rise and influence of the new atheism reminds us that the apologetic task cannot or at least should not be ignored. Nor should it be left solely as the province, Al Schmidt recently argued, of evangelicals.[35] After all, apologetics is, as David Scaer once described it, a necessary and biblical task.[36]

---

[34] Harris, *The End of Faith*, 227.

[35] Alvin J. Schmidt, "Christianity Needs More Lutheran Apologetes," in *Tough-Minded Christianity: Honoring the Legacy of John Warwick Montgomery* (Nashville: B&H Academic, 2008), 495-512.

[36] David P. Scaer, "Apologetics as Theological Discipline: Reflections on a Necessary and Biblical Task," in *Let Christ Be Christ: Theology, Ethics & World Religions in the Two Kingdoms* (Huntington Beach: Tentatio Press, 1999), 299-307.

Does this mean, then, that Lutherans ought to start dabbling in natural theology and proofs for God's existence? An earlier confessional Lutheran theologian, Ernst Hengstenberg, answered in the affirmative when he wrote, just as Darwin was thinking about *Origin of Species*:

> Materialism's appearance has made us aware of the significant deficiencies in the church in the area of scholarship. Modern existentialist theology is totally foreign to apologetic efforts. We are far less equipped than [others] with valid proofs of the truth of revelation and its individual teachings. An overreaction to rationalism has made us lukewarm toward natural theology, which in older times was seen as the necessary underpinning of positive [or confessional] theology. These gaps must necessarily be filled.[37]

Is this still the case today? It seems so. This is not to suggest that theistic proofs ought to be the sole focus, or even the starting point, of our apologetic efforts. Context determines that. Moreover, we know, as C.S. Lewis implied in *Mere Christianity*, that acceptance of theistic proofs doesn't *necessarily* get anyone close to the God of Christianity. We must, however, confess that God can be known to exist by reflecting on nature or the basis of our intuitive moral compass, as marred as it is. Such "natural" starting points might also help the evangelist in communicating to the atheist the law of God, for, as Lewis put it, only after one realizes "that there is a real Moral Law, and a Power behind the law, and that you have broken that law and put yourself wrong with that Power—it's *after* all that that Christianity begins to talk."[38]

So where does this leave us, with not the church's kerygma, but our apologetic? Might I suggest that our apologetic starts where Lutheran apologists have always started, with a positive case for and defense of the incarnation of God in real historical time and real historical space? For if there is a case not just for the existence of God but a real, meaningful, and verifiable revelation from God, it is found, as Antony Flew himself recently intimated, in the historical

---

[37] Quoted in Fredrick Gregory, *Nature Lost: Natural Science and the German Theological Traditions of the Nineteenth Century,* (Cambridge: Harvard University Press, 1992), 116.

[38] Lewis, *Mere Christianity* (New York: Macmillan, 1952), 24.

and theological assertion that God was in Christ reconciling the world unto himself (2 Cor 5:19).[39] Whatever our starting point, though, if we are to address atheism and any other contemporary challenge to the faith, it's high time we get involved in the most necessary and biblical task of Christian apologetics.

---

[39] See especially Flew, *There Is a God*, 185-213.

Postscript

Since I wrote this last essay, the movement known as the new atheism has all but died. Two of its four most vocal proponents—Christopher Hitchens and Daniel Dennett—are deceased. Richard Dawkins recently lamented the slow but steady advance of Islam in Britain and surprised everyone by describing himself as a "cultural Christian." And the last of the four, Sam Harris, is now promoting his version of spiritual-but-not-religious philosophy. None of them were (or are) dummies. True, they never advanced any compelling, positive arguments for atheism. Their criticism of the arguments for God's existence displayed a profound ignorance of modern cosmological, teleological, and ontological arguments for theism. And their dismissal of Christian theism never followed a serious consideration of the historical evidence for Jesus' life, death, and resurrection.

They were, however, good at exposing the problem of fideism. Fideism is the posture some Christians take when they respond to criticisms and objections to Christianity not by appeals to evidence or by offering a reasoned explanation but by merely appealing to their faith that Christianity is true. It presumes that the faith needs no *apologia*, and it reduces the epistemic credibility of Christianity to that of virtually every other world religion. The Bible, however, encourages us to always be prepared to give an *apologia* (1 Pt. 3:15). It tells us that we can know things about the one true God apart from nature. Psalm 19:1, for example, says, "The heavens declare the glory of God, and the sky above proclaims his handiwork." In Romans, Paul argues that "what can be known about God is plain" to all men and women "because God has shown it to them. For his invisible attributes, namely, his eternal power and divine nature, have been clearly perceived, ever since the creation of the world, in the things that have been made" (Rom. 1:19-20).

Natural science is starting to say yes as well. According to Discovery Institute's Stephen C. Meyer's *Return of the God Hypothesis*, three major discoveries of the twentieth century all but make plain the existence of God. Big Bang cosmology posits that the universe had a beginning. It came into existence caused by something other than itself. Additionally, it came into existence and persists in such a way that, despite overwhelming odds against it, permits and sustains life. The universe, and especially our solar system, is, in fact, finely tuned for life. Lastly, and most remarkably, molecular biology discovered that behind every living organism is a genetic code that is immeasurably more advanced than the code in the most sophisticated computer software.

The details of Meyer's argument are more than impressive. He doesn't prove God's existence in the formal deductive sense—the way that, for example, William Lane Craig's kalām cosmological argument does. What Meyer shows, though, is that the more scientists investigate nature, the more the theistic worldview makes sense. In fact, given the other options—from atheism to pantheism—it's the one that best explains what is behind nature. He writes:

> The press of this evidence upon our scientific awareness suggests that we do not need to…accept God's existence as a mere philosophical necessity. Instead, reflecting on this evidence can enable us to discover—or rediscover—the reality of God. And that discovery is good news indeed. We are not alone in a vast impersonal and meaningless universe—the product of 'blind, pitiless indifference.'

This is what Dawkins concludes (and presumes). "Instead," continues Meyer, "the evidence points to a personal intelligence behind the physical world that we observe."[1]

What else might nature and the natural sciences tell us? Darwinian biological evolution tells us that we descended from apes—that we are the product of long and undirected evolutionary

---

[1] Stephen C. Meyer, *The Return of the God Hypothesis: Three Scientific Discoveries that Reveal the Mind Behind the Universe* (New York: Harper One, 2020), 449-450.

processes. That's one hypothesis. It might explain some features of the human animal, but it fails miserably in explaining others. For example, it cannot explain where the information that directs cellular replication came from. Neither can it account for the irreducible complexity of the various organ systems of the human body. A close look at the physical nature of human beings demonstrates that we are indeed fearfully and wonderfully made (Ps. 139:14). What nature can't tell us, though, is what we were ultimately made for. Yes, we might know some penultimate things such as the vocations we find ourselves in through basic biological functions like father or motherhood. These and our other vocations give us purpose, but such a purpose is in the here and now. We might sense that purpose extends past our natural lives, but nature can't really reveal what that is.

Nature is cruel like that. It may reveal some things about us and even point beyond itself to something higher. It can't tell us much more, though, and there will always be other ways of explaining things. After all, nature doesn't speak. We speak for it as we describe what we see. Some explanations are better than others, but they remain our explanations—except if we had some perspective from outside, above, and behind nature. Even better would be if the author of nature provided an explanation. And he has. He spoke the universe into existence. He spoke through prophets. Two thousand years ago, he spoke through his son Jesus of Nazareth (Heb. 1:1-2).

Who was this man? His disciples asked the same question: "What sort of man is this, that even winds and sea obey him?" (Matt. 8:27). He controlled nature. He calmed the sea. He turned water into wine and healed the sick. And yet, he seemed like just a man. He cried, ate when he got hungry, rested when he was tired, and, in the end, died just like any other man. But even in death, something was a bit different. As he hung on the cross, darkness settled across the land. When he uttered his last words, nature responded. The "earth shook, and the rocks split" (Matt. 27:51). (Even the second- and third-century Greco-Roman historians, Phlagon of Caria and Thallus, took note of both the darkness and earthquakes that happened.[2]) Three days later,

---

[2] See Paul L. Maier, *The Genuine Jesus: Fresh Evidence from History and Archeology* (Grand Rapids: Kregel Pulbications, 2021), 241-242; Robert E. Van Voorst, *Jesus Outside the New Testament: An Introduction to the Ancient*

after his lifeless body had been laid in a tomb that was sealed shut by a stone, an earthquake caused it to roll away. And when his disciples saw him raised from the dead, they remembered how he had said he would do just this, for this was the promise concerning the Messiah in Scripture, so "they believed the Scripture" (John 2:22). Why? Because the Scripture is where God spoke in the past. Jesus called it—the books comprising the Old Testament—the very word of God (Mark 7:3). He also promised that he and the Father would send the Holy Spirit to the apostles (John 14 and 16). He would cause them to remember everything that Jesus taught them and would inspire their teaching and preaching, which would eventually be written down and comprise the New Testament. It is here where God reveals himself, the character of creation and his human creatures both in his condemnation of it and the good news that he would one day, in Christ, reconcile it all unto himself.

There is much more to the apologetic task today than what is covered in these essays. This is, in many ways, reflective of the nature of thinking and practicing apologetics today. Contexts and their respective challenges are always changing and evolving. When Paul traveled through mid-first-century Athens, Jewish, Epicurean, and Stoic objections to Christianity were the challenges. In twenty-first-century America, they are all over the map—from the practical atheism of secularism to the gelatinous ramblings of spiritual-but-not-religious people. Apologetics requires intellectual flexibility. It also requires study. I hope the foregoing essays will get the ball rolling.

Evidence (Grand Rapids, Wm. B. Eerdmans-Lightning Source, 2000), 20–21; Jennifer Viegas, "Quake Reveals Day of Jesus' Crucifixion," *NBC News,* May 24, 2012, https://www.nbcnews.com/id/wbna47555983.

General Index

Scriptural Index

2 Corinthians, 5:19, 115
Hebrews, 1:1-2, 27, 119
1 Peter, 3:15, vii, 42, 117
2 Peter
    1:20, 10
    3:16, vii, 10

Early Christian Writings

Apostolic Fathers

1 Clement, 42:3, 65n29

Lutheran Works

Luther's Works (LW)
    1:25, 50n33
    25:430, 43n13
    26:29-30, 42n11
    26:30, 51n36
    30:105, 42n12
    45:200-201, 43n14
    45:208, 44n16
    45:213, 44n18
    47:300, 45n21
    47:305-306, 45n22

Weimar Ausgabe (WA)
    30/2:185, 46nn24–25
    53:278, 47n28
    53:284, 47n29
    53:378, 47n30
    53:572, 51n37

Islamic Literature

Qur'an
    2:30, 87
    2:37, 18

2:37-38, 88
2:38-39, 18
2:216, 74, 91
2:256, 90–91
3:3, 99
3:3-4, 89
3:45, 23
3:47, 24
3:59, 24
3:64-73, 80n36
3:64ff, 19
3:83, 73
4:157, 99
4:171, 21, 23, 48, 90, 98
5:3, 19
5:82-83, 80n37
5:110, 97–98
6:164, 99
7:11-12, 87
7:54-60, 86
7:172, 74
8:39, 91
9:5, 90, 91
9:16-33, 97
9:29, 82
9:29-33, 98
9:30, 90
9:33, 74
17:19-25, 87
17:26, 87
19:35, 90
19:89, 90
19:92, 90
25:1, 25
61:6, 19, 98
72:3, 90
112:1-4, 85, 89

More Best Sellers from

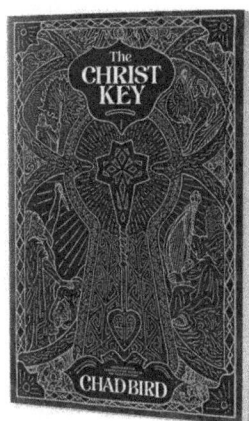

1517.

Never Go Another Day Without Hearing the Gospel of Jesus.

Visit **www.1517.org**
for free Gospel resources.